中国当代书画名家作品收藏指南

孟云飞 著
李福生 译

中央编译出版社
Central Compilation & Translation Press

当代中国书画名家作品收藏指南编辑委员会

名　誉　主　任：高占祥
名誉副主任：王　琦　沈　鹏
执　行　主　任：刘　艺
副　　主　　任：吕立新　刘金富　王立文
艺　术　顾　问：白雪石　廖静文　赵长青　李　铎　姚治华　米景扬
　　　　　　　　张旭光　邹德忠　田伯平　梅墨生　李洪海　李　涵
　　　　　　　　李元茂　史希光　董辰生　石晓玲
编　　　　委：张铜彦　张瑞祥　张金卫　夏国珠　顾　莹　鲁　闽
　　　　　　　　韩振刚　张　敢　李家骝　吴守峰　缪法宝　翟品善
　　　　　　　　何学斌　郭利杰　杨　军　王立文　周佳洁　高　菲
　　　　　　　　索之华　张雯君　孙振宇
主　　　　编：孟云飞
副　　主　　编：袁　睿　朱　清
摄　　　　影：曹　云
责　任　编　辑：程　宇
责　任　校　对：周　钊

序 言

中华民族文明的历程，于今已达数千年之久了。中国书画作为民族文化艺术的重要部分，为促进人类文明和社会进步发挥了巨大的历史作用。独特的中国书画艺术，造就了许许多多伟大的艺术巨匠，他们为我们留下了极其丰富的艺术瑰宝。

胡锦涛总书记在中国文联第八次全国代表大会、中国作协第七次全国代表大会上指出："全面建设小康社会、开创中国特色社会主义新局面的历史进程必将推动我国文艺事业全面发展繁荣，中华民族的伟大复兴必将伴随着中华文化的伟大复兴。"建国后，尤其是改革开放三十年来，社会稳定，国民经济飞速发展，党和政府对文化建设的高度重视，促使了文化艺术产业的大力发展。人民群众生活水平随着经济的发展，得到了很大的提高，收藏书画艺术作品已经成为很多人尤其是企业家、收藏家重要的文化生活内容。艺术品市场已经成为不可或缺的投资市场之一。

为了让广大书画爱好者及企业家、收藏家更好更准确地了解把握书画艺术品市场，了解书画家的艺术风格、特点、市场认知度及收藏价值，提高书画收藏的水平，我们特邀请了全国著名书画艺术家、文化部文化艺术评估委员会的专家以及拍卖行业的专家，组织编撰了《当代中国书画名家作品收藏指南》一书，供社会广大书画艺术品投资者、企业家、收藏家参考。

白雪石 BAI XUESHI

白雪石 1915年6月12日生，中国现代著名国画家，生于古都北京一个普通的市民家庭，原名增锐，斋号何须斋，中国美术家协会会员，北京山水画研究会会长。

润笔价格：150000~180000/平尺
供收藏家参考

Bai Xueshi, born on June 12th, 1915, in a common family in Beijing, is a famous contemporary traditional Chinese painter. Previously known as Bai Zengrui and with his study as Hexu Study, he is a member of China Artists Association and Director of Landscape Painting Research Society of Beijing.

Reference Price: RMB 150,000-180,000 per square feet

《漓江渔家》96*180
Fishing Family at Lijiang River

中国当代书画名家作品收藏指南

《顺风行舟》97*180 feetSailing Downwind

缪法宝 MIU FABAO

缪法宝 1936年生，教授，现为中国美术家协会会员，中国书法家协会会员，一级创作员，国家文化部艺术委员，国家人事部一级艺术委员，中国国际新闻出版社书画院副院长、艺委会主任、徐悲鸿画院名誉院长。

润笔价格：40000~50000/平尺
供收藏家参考

Professor Liao Fabao, born in 1963, is a National Class A artist, member of China Artists Association and China Calligraphers Association, member of Arts Committee of Ministry of Culture, Class A member of Arts Committee of Ministry of Human Resources and Social Security, Vice President and Director of Arts Committee of Calligraphy and Painting Gallery of China International News Press, and Honorary President of Xu Beihong Gallery.

Reference price: RMB 40,000-50,000 per square

范扬 FAN YANG

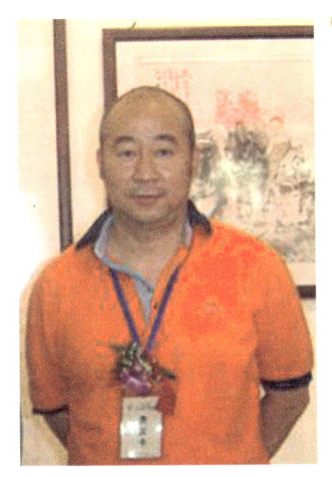

范　扬　1955年生于香港，祖籍江苏南通市，南京师范大学美术学院教授，博士生导师，中国美术家协会会员。

润笔价格：40000~50000/平尺
供收藏家参考

with his ancestral home in Nantong, Jiangsu Province, and born in Hong Kong in 1955, is a professor and PhD supervisor at Academy of Fine Arts, Nanjing Normal University, and member of China Artists Association.

Reference price: RMB 40,000-50,000 per square feet

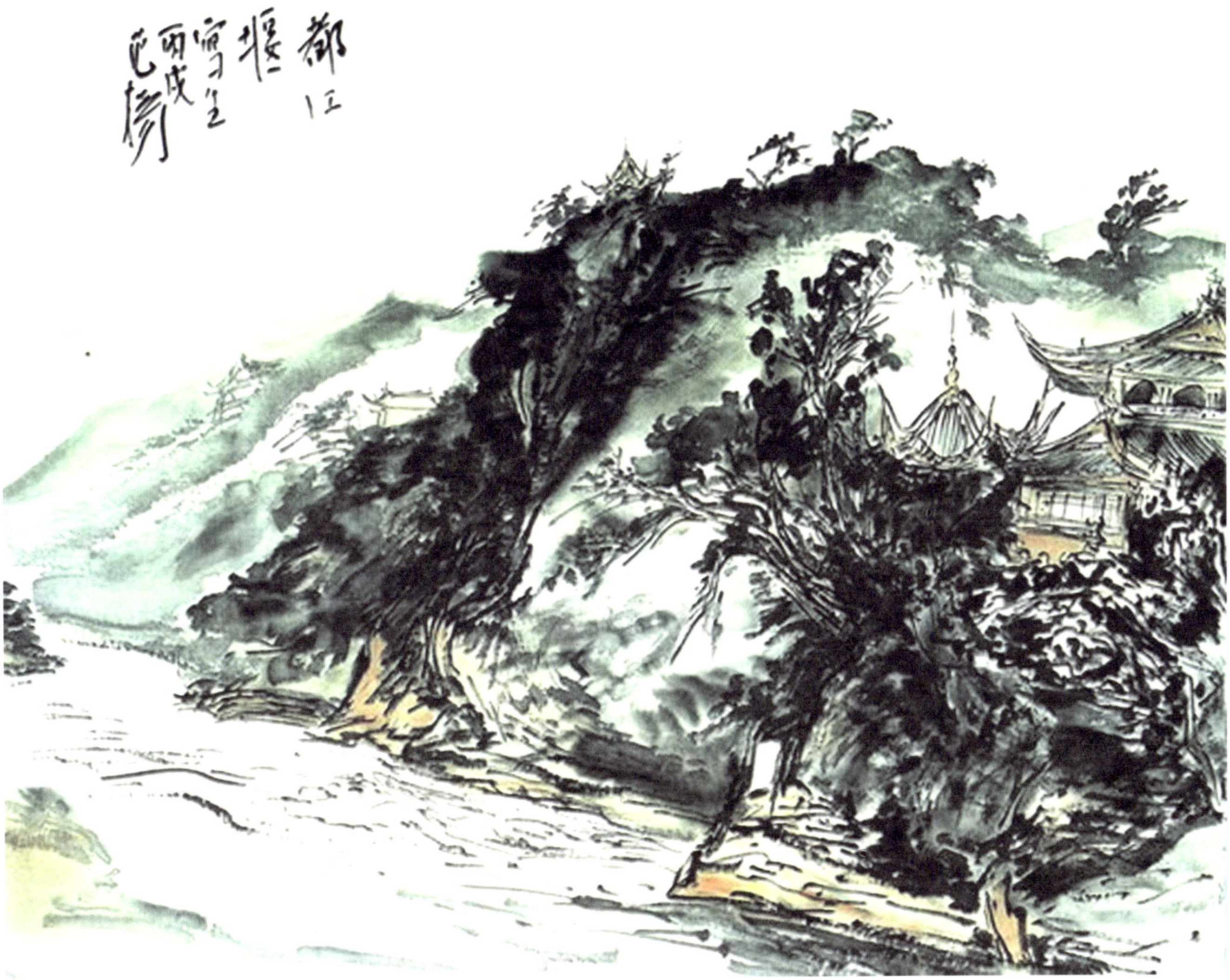

《都江堰》 *Dujiang Weir*

《旭日迎辉》97*180 Rising Sun

何学斌
HE XUEBIN

何学斌 中国和谐东方书画艺术研究院院长，国家一级美术师，中国美术家协会会员。

润笔价格：40000~50000/平尺
供收藏家参考

He Xuebin is President of Harmonious Research Institute of Oriental Calligraphy and Painting, National Class A artist of fine arts, and member of China Artists Association.

Reference price: RMB 40,000-50,000 per square feet

董辰生
DONG CHENSHENG

《欢乐的塔吉克》 *Happy Tajik Girl*

董辰生 1929 生，原名秉宸，《解放军画报》社美术编辑，中国美协理事，中国美协第三、四届理事。

润笔价格：25000~30000/ 平尺
供收藏家参考

Dong Chensheng, born in 1929 and formerly known as Dong Bingchen, is an art editor at PLA Pictorial. Dong was a council member of the third and fourth session of China Arts Association.

Reference price: RMB 25,000-30,000 per square feet

《五莲山》240*110 Five-lotus Mountain

孙长武
SUN CHANGWU

孙长武　画名南山河，号东山樵夫，南山画社创始人，南阳市美协副主席，南阳市收藏家协会秘书长，安徽省美术家协会会员。现为中国国家画院张志民工作室专职画家。

润笔价格：10000~15000/平尺
供收藏家参考

Sun Changwu, with Nanshanhe (South Mountain and River) and Woodsman on East Mountain as his literary names, is the founding father of Nanshan Painting Gallery. Sun is Vice President of Nanyang Artists Association, Secretary General of Nanyang Association of Collectors, member of Anhui Artists Association, and a professional painter with Zhang Zhimin Studio of China National Academy of Painting.

Reference price: RMB 10,000-15,000 per square feet

《湘西芙蓉镇即景》 A Sketch of Furong Town in West Hunan

程振国 （1946.2—）山东临朐人，号若痴，中国美术家协会理事，北京美协艺委会委员，北京海淀书画院副院长。

润笔价格：15000~20000/平尺
供收藏家参考

Cheng Zhenguo, born in Linqu, Shandong Province, in February 1946, and with Ruo Chi as his literary name, is a council member of China Artists Association, member of Arts Committee of Beijing Artists Association, and Vice President of Haidian Calligraphy and Painting Gallery of Beijing.

Reference price: RMB 15,000-20,000 per square feet

石晓玲 SHI XIAOLING

石晓玲 1962年出生，江苏扬州人，全国青联委员，北京市政协委员，民革委员，中国书法艺术研究院艺委会主任。

润笔价格：15000~20000/平尺
供收藏家参考

Shi Xiaoling, born in 1962 in Yangzhou, Jiangsu Province, is a member of All-China Youth Federation, member of Beijing Municipal Committee of CPPCC, member of Revolutionary Committee of Chinese Kuomintang, and Director of Arts Committee of China Calligraphy Research Institute.

Reference Price: RMB 15,000-20,000 per square feet

《荷塘清香》180*97

《华穗迎秋》 *Autumn Harvest*

霍春阳
HUO CHUNYANG

霍春阳　1946年生，现任天津美术学院中国画系系主任、教授，天津美术学院美术馆馆长，中国美术家协会会员，中国书法家协会会员，天津美术家协会副主席，天津青年美协顾问。

润笔价格：35000~40000/平尺
供收藏家参考

Professor Huo Chunyang, born in 1946, is Dean of Department of Traditional Chinese Painting and Curator of Art Gallery in Tianjin Academy of Fine Arts, member of China Artists Association and of China Calligraphers Association, Vice President of Tianjin Artists Association, and consultant for Tianjin Young Artists Association.

Reference price: RMB 35,000-40,000 per square feet

《五福》97*180 Five Melons of Happiness

刘岳林
LIU YUELIN

刘岳林 曾用名刘克敏，汉族，1950年，中国书画家协会副主席，中国艺术品价值评审委员会副主任，中国哈密瓜艺术研究院院长。

润笔价格：15000~25000/平尺

供收藏家参考

Liu Yuelin, born in 1950 and formerly known as Liu Kemin, is Vice President of China Calligrapher and Painter Association, Vice Director of Chinese Art Ware Appraisal Committee, and President of Melon Art Institute of China.

Reference price: RMB 15,000-20,000 per square feet

焦可群 JIAO KEQUN

焦可群 1930年生于陕西西安，中国美术家协会会员，中国老教授协会会员，中央美术学院中国画系学术顾问，中国书画函授大学教授，中国老年书画研究会创作指导委员会委员。

润笔价格：25000~30000/平尺
供收藏家参考

Jiao Kequn, born in Xi'an, Shaanxi Province, in 1930, is a member of China Artists Association and of China Senior Professors Association, a consultant of Department of Traditional Chinese Painting in Central Academy of Fine Arts, professor at China Painting and Calligraphy Correspondence University, and member of Instruction Committee of China Calligraphy and Arts Research Institute for Seniors.

Reference price: RMB 25,000-30,000 per square feet

《秋山回眸》 *A Glimpse of Mountain in Autumn*

陈洪军
CHEN HUNJUN

陈洪军 1957年8月生，北京山水画会理事，白雪石艺术研究会副会长，北京水墨画研究会副秘书长，中国人民对外友好协会艺术创作院副秘书长。

润笔价格：15000~20000/平尺
供收藏家参考

Chen Hongjun, born in Beijing in August 1957, is a council member of Landscape Painting Research Society of Beijing, Vice President of Bai Xueshi Research Institute, Vice Secretary-General of Beijing Ink and Wash Painting Research Institute, and Vice Secretary-General of Art Gallery of Chinese People's Association for Friendship with Foreign Countries.

Reference price: RMB 15,000-20,000 per square feet

《漓江早春》96*180 *Lijiang River in Early Spring*

李荣海
LI RONGHAI

《乾坤清风图》 Breeze

李荣海 现为中国美术家协会分党组成员副秘书长，中国美术家协会理事，中国书法家协会理事，中国白洋淀诗书画院名誉院长，中国书画印研究院专家委员，中央机关书画协会副主席，中国书法家协会评审委员、研究馆员。

润价笔格：25000~30000/平尺
供收藏家参考

Li Ronghai is a sub-committee member of the CPC committee at China Artists Association and Vice Secretary General of CAA, council member of China Artists Association and of China Calligraphers Association, Honorary President of Baiyangdian Gallery of China, expert member of Calligraphy, Painting and Seal Research Institute of China, Vice President of Calligraphy and Painting Association of Central Organs of the CPC, and member of the Appraisal Committee and researcher of China Calligraphers Association.

Reference price: RMB 25,000-30,000 per square feet

孙玉国 SUN YUGUO

孙玉国 笔名石磊，中国美术家协会会员，中国三峡画院副院长，艺委会主任，中国现代绘画艺术研究院副院长，中国山水画研究会理事，

润笔价格：10000~15000/平尺
供收藏家参考

Sun Yuguo, with Shi Lei as his literary name, is a member of China Artists Association, Vice President of Three Gorges Art Gallery of China, Director of Art Committee of Three Gorges Art Gallery of China, Vice President of Modern Painting Research Institute of China, and council member of China Landscape Paining Research Association.

Reference price: RMB 10,000-15,000 per square feet

《仙山揽胜图》 96*180 *A Panoramic View of Divine Mountain*

《天开图画》 Picture of World Creation

梅墨生
MEI MOSHENG

梅墨生 1960生，现为中国国家画院理论研究部副主任，院艺委会委员，国家一级美术师，中国书法家协会会员，中国美术家协会会员，现为文化部艺术品评估委员会委员，文化部国家艺术科研课题项目评审专家，《20世纪美术作品国家档案》艺术委员会委员，中国文物学会特聘专家。

润笔价格：40000~50000/平尺
供收藏家参考

Mei Mosheng, born in 1960, is a National Class A artist, Vice Director of Department of Theoretical Research at China National Academy of Painting and member of Art Committee of the academy, and member of China Calligraphers Association and of China Artists Association. Mei is also a member of Art Ware Appraisal Committee and expert assessor of National Arts Research Project of Ministry of Culture, member of Arts Committee of National Archives of 20th Century Works of Fine Arts, and a distinguished expert of China Cultural Relics Association.

Reference price: RMB 40,000-50,000 per square feet

魏斗
WEI DOU

魏 斗 1960年生，现为中央书画院院士，中华书画委员会副秘书长，中国诗书画研究院美术研究员，北京美协会员。

润笔价格：8000~10000/平尺
供收藏家参考

Wei Dou, born in 1960, is a painter with Central Calligraphy and Painting Institute, Vice Secretary-General of Calligraphy and Painting Commission of China, researcher with Chinese Poetry, Calligraphy, and Painting Institute, and member of Beijing Artists Association.

Reference price: RMB 8,000-10,000 per square feet

《竹报平安节节高》
Bamboo

《柿柿如意》 Happiness of Persimmon

米景扬 （1936——）北京人（祖籍浙江省绍兴市），文化部文化市场发展中心艺术品评估委员会委员，绘画雕塑工作委员会主任，荣宝斋艺术顾问，中国美术家协会会员等。

润笔价格：30000~35000/平尺
供收藏家参考

Mi Jingyang, born in Beijing (with his ancestral home in Shaoxing, Zhejiang Province) in 1936, is a member of Art Ware Appraisal Committee of Art Development Center under Ministry of Culture, Director of Painting and Sculpture Committee, Art Consultant of Rong Bao Zhai, and member of China Artists Association.

Reference price: RMB 30,000-35,000 per square feet

翟品善
ZHAI PINSHAN

翟品善　国画家及篆刻艺术家，首批获"国务院政府特殊贡献津贴"，奖励的国家级专家，国家人事部授予"著名国画艺术家"称号。

润笔价格：35000~40000/平尺

供收藏家参考

Zhai Pinshan is a traditional Chinese painter and seal-cutting artist. He is among the first batch of state-level experts receiving Special Allowance of State Council of China and has the title of Renowned Traditional Chinese Painter.

Reference price: RMB 35,000-40,000 per square feet

《冰清玉洁》180*97

Crystalline and Immaculate

王挥春
WANG HUICHUN

王挥春　笔名涛石，男，1929年生于北京，北京画院专业画家，一级美术师，中国美术家协会会员，中国延安文艺学会会员，中国画研究会研究员兼常务理事，北京湖社画会会长，齐白石艺术研究会常务理事，北京国际艺术博览会评审委员会副主任，中国书画函授大学教授。

润笔价格：25000~30000/平尺
供收藏家参考

Wang Huichun, with Tao Shi as his literary name, was born in Beijing in 1929. A National Class A professional painter with Beijing Fine Art Academy, Wang is member of Yan'an Literature and Art Society of China, researcher and standing council member of Chinese Painting Research Institute, Director of Beijing Hushe Painting Society, standing council member of Qi Baishi Research Institute, Vice Director of Review Committee of Beijing International Art Expo, and professor with China Calligraphy and Painting Correspondence University.

Reference price: RMB 25,000-30,000 per square feet

《松鹰图》 *Picture of Pine and Eagl*

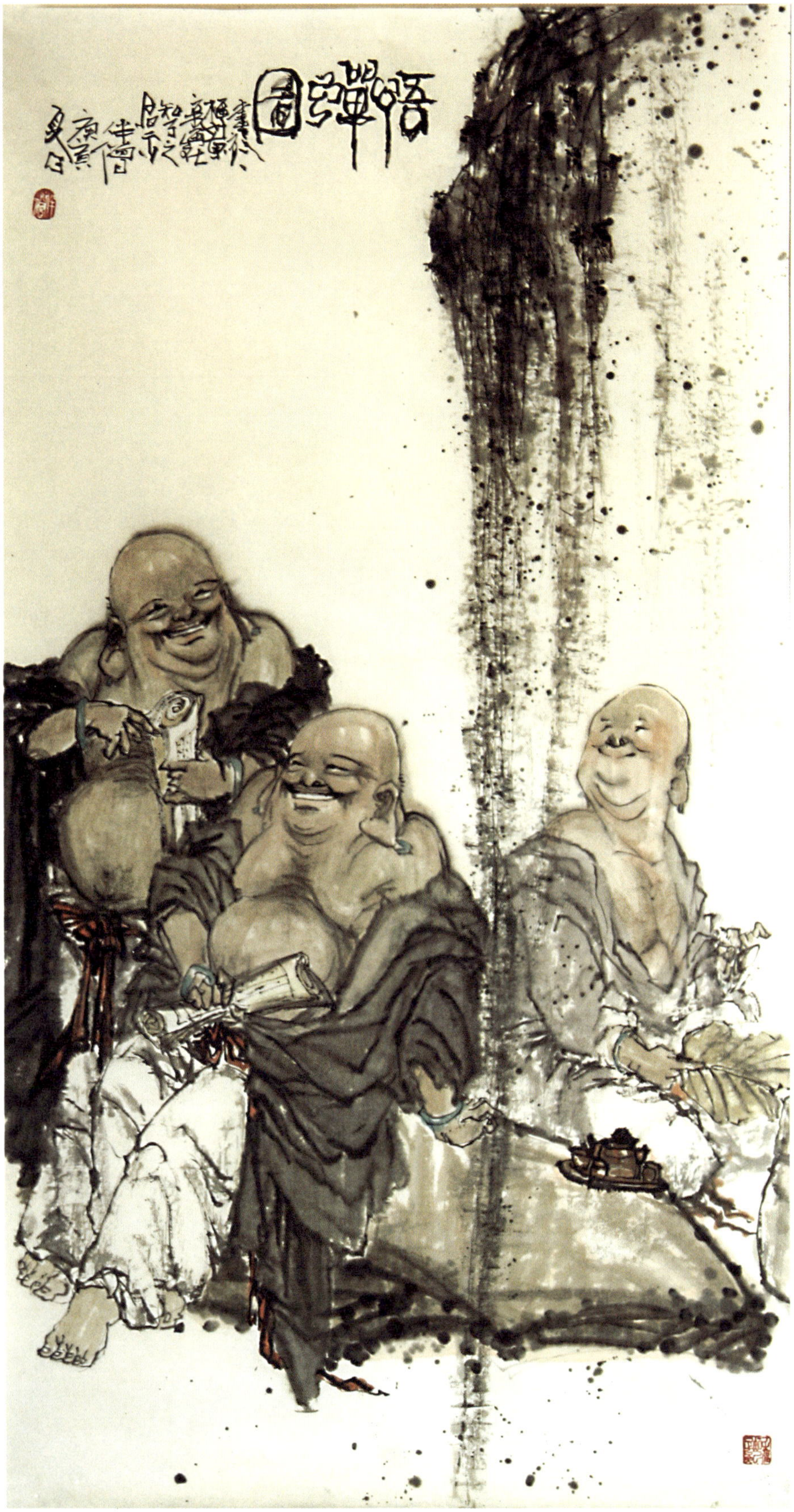

《悟禅图》180*97 *Understanding Zen*

陈振国 CHEN ZHENGUO

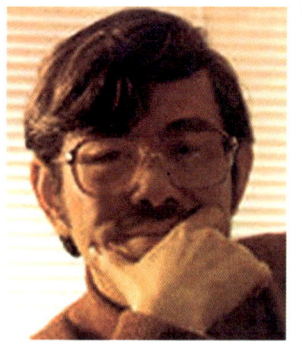

陈振国 1945年生于福建福州，中国美术家协会会员，中国画家协会理事，中国书法美术家创作中心终身教授。

润笔价格：4000~5000/平尺
供收藏家参考

Chen Zhenguo, born in Fuzhou, Fujian Province, in 1945, is a member of China Artists Association, standing council member of China Calligrapher and Painter Association, and life tenured professor with Creative Center of China Calligraphers and Artists of Fine Arts.

Reference price: RMB 4,000-5,000 per square feet

《南方古镇》系列之八 / No. 8 of Ancient Towns in South China Series

王　琦　中央美术学院教授，历任中国版画家协会秘书长，副主席、主席，中国美术家协会理事，常务理事、副主席、党组书记、顾问。

润笔价格：150000~180000/平尺

供收藏家参考

Wang Qi, a professor with Central Academy of Fine Arts, has served as Secretary General, Vice President, and President of China Printmakers Associations, and Standing Council Member, Vice President, Party Secretary, and Consultant of China Artists Association.

Reference price: RMB 150,000-180,000 per square feet

《前程似锦》98*180 Bright Prospects

唐明芳 TANG MINGFANG

唐明芳 1969年生，现为中国国画家协会理事，一级画师，中国书法美术艺术创作中心副教授。

润笔价格：8000~12000/平尺
供收藏家参考

Tang Mingfang, born in 1969, is a National Class A painter, council member with China Association of Traditional Chinese Painting, and assistant professor with Creative Center of China Calligraphers and Artists of Fine Arts.

Reference price: RMB 8,000-12,000 per square feet

《李清照诗意》
Poetic Essence of Li Qingzhao

王西京
WANG XIJING

王西京 男，1946年8月生于西安，汉族，中共党员，国家级有突出贡献专家，国家一级美术师，西安中国画院院长。陕西省美术家协会主席。

润笔价格：30000~35000/平尺
供收藏家参考

Wang Xijing, born in Xi'an in August 1946 and of Han nationality, is a Party member, state-level expert with outstanding contribution, National Class A artist of fine arts, President of Xi'an Traditional Chinese Painting Academy and of Shaanxi Artists Association.

Reference price: RMB 30,000-35,000 per square feet

《正气满人间》97*180 *Ubiquitous Uprightness*

黄明铭
HUANG MINGMING

黄明铭 1941年10月生于福建漳州，中国书画家协会常务副主席，新加坡中华美术研究会永久会员，新加坡中华文化艺术交流中心副主任，新加坡《星中国际美术》永久副主席。

润笔价格：8000~10000/平尺
供收藏家参考

Huang Mingming, born in Zhangzhou, Fujian Province, in October 1941, is standing Vice President of China Calligrapher and Painter Association, life member of Singapore Society of Chinese Artists, Vice Director of Singapore Exchanges Center of Chinese Culture and Art, and tenured Vice President of Singapore-China International Art.

Reference price: RMB 8,000-10,000 per square feet

姚少华 YAO SHAOHUA

姚少华 1942年8月生，现为中国书画名人联合会副会长，被聘为中国文联，中国文艺网等多家艺术团体顾问。

润笔价格：20000~25000/平尺
供收藏家参考

Yao Shaohua, born in August 1942, is Vice President of Federation of Master Traditional Chinese Painters and Calligraphers. He is also a consultant of many art groups such as China Federation of Literary and Art Circles and China Literature and Art Network

Reference price: RMB 20,000-25,000 per square feet

《长白雄风》 *Tiger at Changbai Mountain*

郝志国 HAO ZHIGUO

郝志国 男，1944年生，中国美术家协会会员，中国版画家协会理事，大同大学美术教授，中国优秀版画家鲁迅奖获得者。

润笔价格：12000~16000/平尺
供收藏家参考

Hao Zhiguo, male, born in 1944, is a member of China Artists Association, council member of China Printmakers Association, fine art professor with Datong University, and winner of Lu Xun Prize for Excellent Printmakers in China.

Reference price: RMB 12,000-16,000 per square feet

《紫气东来图》96*170　Propitious Omen

《翡翠谷春雨》 Spring Rain at Jade Valley

姚治华 当代著名画家，1932年9月2日出生，中央美术学院毕业后留校任教，曾先后任助教、讲师、教授、中华英才艺术研究院院长、中国画系教研室副主任、主任、教授等。

润笔价格：30000~40000/平尺
供收藏家参考

姚治华
YAO ZHIHUA

Yao Zhihua, born on September 2nd, 1932, is a famous contemporary painter. After graduation from Central Academy of Fine Arts, he has been teaching in the school as an assistant teacher, lecturer, assistant professor, and now President of Top China Art Academy, and Dean and Professor with Department of Traditional Chinese Painting.

Reference price: RMB 30,000-40,000 per square feet

陈友旺
CHEN YOUWANG

陈友旺 男,1948年11月19日生,国家一级演员北京市戏剧家协会会员,中国乡土艺术协会会员,世界书画艺术评介协会会员,炎黄书画家协会常务理事。

润笔价格：6000~8000/ 平尺
供收藏家参考

《野猪林》 Wild Boar Fores

Chen Youwang, male, born on November 19th, 1948, is a National Class A actor, member of Beijing Dramatists Association, of China Association of Local Arts, and World Calligraphy and Painting Association, and standing council member of Yanhuang Association of Calligraphers and Painters.

Reference price: RMB 6,000-8,000 per square feet

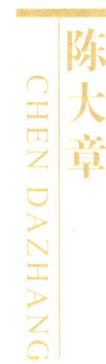

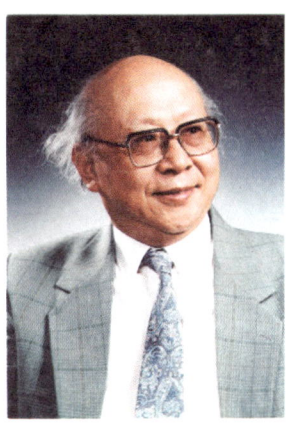

陈大章　1930 年出生于书画世家，现为中国美术家协会会员，北京海峡两岸书画研究会会长，文化部老艺术家书画社社长，中国工艺美术协会国画研究会会长。

润笔价格：40000~50000/ 平尺
供收藏家参考

陈大章
CHEN DAZHANG

Chen Dazhang, born in a painter's family in 1930, is a member of China Artists Association, President of Beijing Cross-strait Research Institute of Calligraphy and Painting, Director of Calligraphy and Painting Studio for Senior Artists of Ministry of Culture, President of Traditional Chinese Painting Research Institute of China Arts and Crafts Association.

Reference price: RMB 40,000-50,000 per square feet

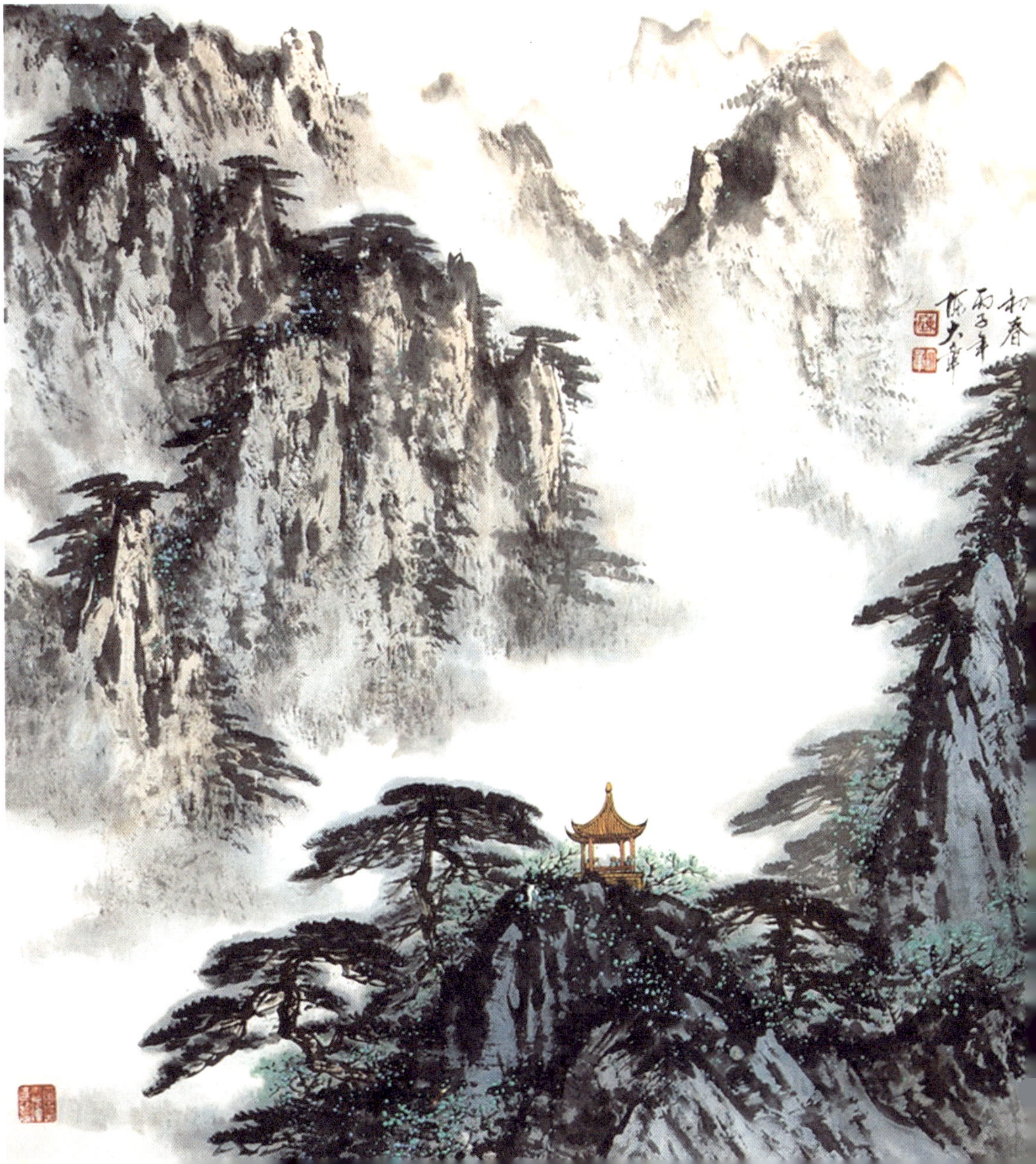

《黄山初春》
Early Spring in Mount. Huangshan

《华夏四季春常在》180*97
Spring Stays through Year in China

孙不俊 男，汉族，中国书画家协会理事，中国神州书画家协会副秘书长，甘肃省书画研究院理事（研究员），徐悲鸿书画研究院副秘书长。

润笔价格：4000~5000/平尺
供收藏家参考

Sun Pijun, of Han nationality, is a council member of China Calligrapher and Painter Association, Vice Secretary General of China Shenzhou Calligrapher and Painter Association, council member (researcher) of Calligraphy and Painting Research Institute of Gansu, and Vice Secretary General of Xu Beihong Research Institute.

Reference Price: RMB 4,000-5,000 per square feet

于志学　冰雪山水画创始人，现任黑龙江省画院名誉院长，第九届全国政协委员，中国美协理事，中国艺术研究院美术创作院创作研究员，中国国际书画艺术研究会副会长，一级美术师。

润笔价格 40000~50000/ 平尺
供收藏家参考

于志学
YU ZHIXUE

Yu Zhixue, founding father of snow-related landscape painting, is a National Class A artist, Honorary President of Heilongjiang Art Academy, council member of China Artists Association, researcher with School of Fine Arts of Chinese National Academy of Arts, and Vice President of China International Association of Painting and Calligraphy. He was also a member of National Committee of the 9th CPPCC.

Reference price: RMB 40,000-50,000 per square feet

《冰雪嬉戏》 Playing with Snow

蔡 超
CAI CHAO

蔡 超 1966年生，中国书画创作基地常务副秘书长，中国金都画院院士，世界华侨华人社团联合总会（艺委会）理事，中国西部画院院长。

润笔价格：6000~8000/平尺
供收藏家参考

Cai Chao, born in 1966, is the standing Vice Secretary General of China Calligraphy and Painting Creation Base, member of China Jindu Art Gallery, council member of Arts Committee of World Federation of Overseas Chinese Associations, and President of West China Art Academy.

Reference price: RMB 6,000-8,000 per square feet
供收藏家参考

《庄子》137*67 *Chuang Tzu*

陈宗麟 男，1942年生，黑龙江美协会员，齐齐哈尔大学教授。

润笔价格：4000~6000/平尺
供收藏家参考

Chen Zonglin, born in 1942, is a member of Heilongjiang Artists Association and professor with Qiqihar University.

Reference price: RMB 4,000-6,000 per square feet
供收藏家参考

《面壁图》 180*97
Wall-facing Meditation

中国当代书画名家作品收藏指南

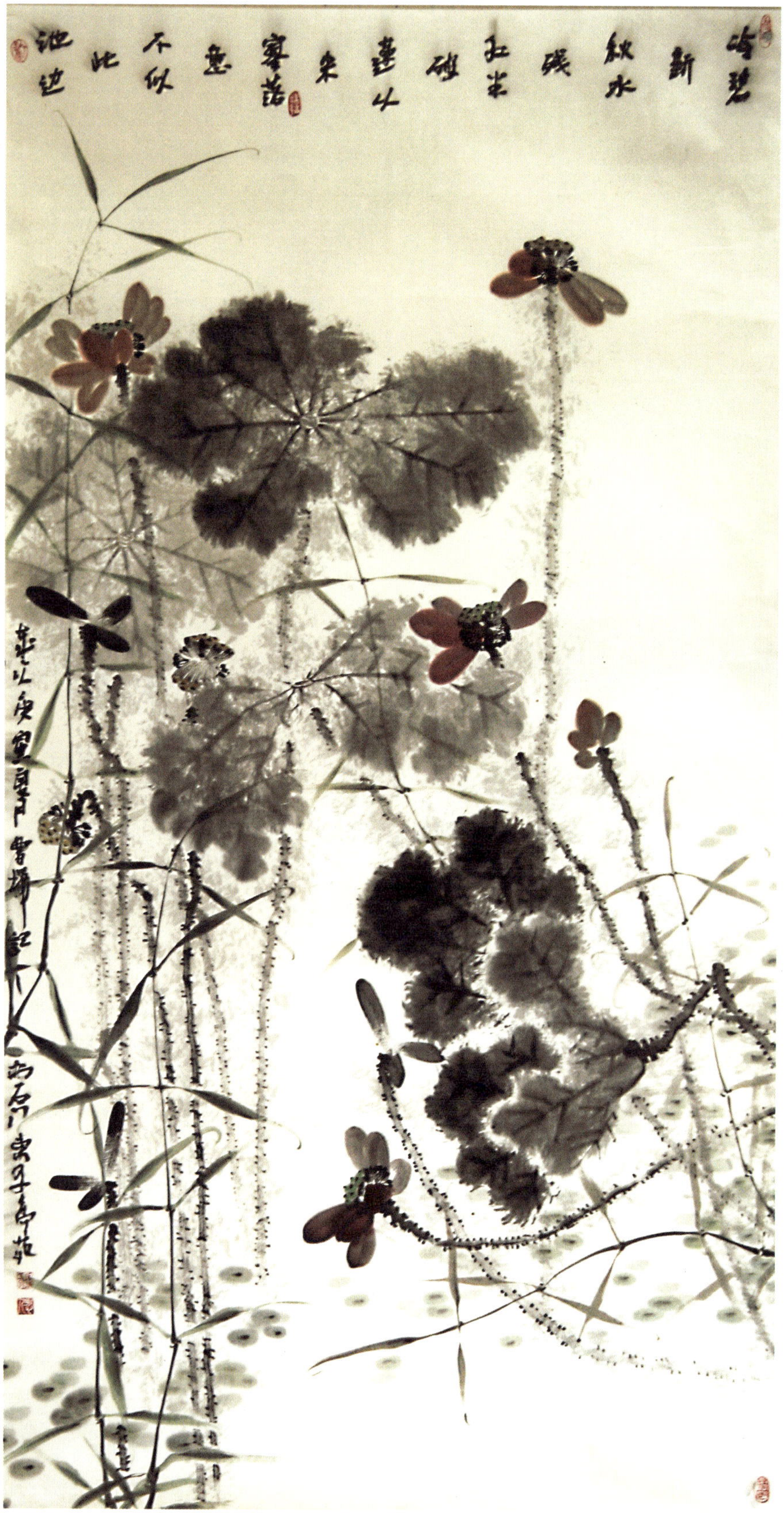

《冷碧新秋水》180*97　*Cold and Clean Water in New Autumn*

曹瑞

CAO RU

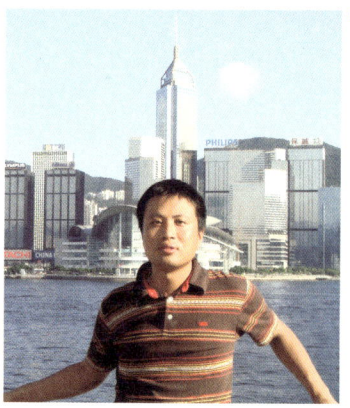

曹　瑞　男，1975年生，中国书画家协会会员。

润笔价格：4000~6000/平尺
供收藏家参考

Cao Rui, male and born in 1975, is a member of China Calligrapher and Painter Association.

Reference price: RMB 4,000-6,000 per square feet

程振铎
CHENG ZHENDUO

程振铎 男,1956年出生于北京,中国文联艺术交流中心创作员,中国新闻国际出版社书画院理事,国家人事部一级艺术委员,中国美术家协会会员。

润笔价格:10000~15000/平尺
供收藏家参考

Chen Zhenduo, born in Beijing in 1956, is a creative member of Art Exchange Center of China Federation of Literary and Art Circles, council member of Calligraphy and Painting Gallery of China International News Press, Class A member of Arts Committee of Ministry of Human Resources and Social Security, and member of China Artists Association.

Reference price: RMB 10,000-15,000 per square feet

《忆江南》97*180 Recalling the South of Yangtze River

《报春图》97*180 *Harbinger of Spring*

代永胜　1945年生于山东，中国民族书画院一级美术师，中国书画家联谊会会员。

润笔价格：3000~6000/平尺
供收藏家参考

代永胜
DAI SHUISHENG

Dai Yongsheng, born in Shandong Province in 1945, is Class A artist of China National Calligraphy and Painting Academy and member of China Calligrapher and Painter Federation.

Reference price: RMB 3,000-6,000 per square feet

樊大牛
FAN DANIU

樊大牛 北空蓝天国画院副院长，中外民间文艺交流促进会篆刻艺术委员会主任，北京民族书画研究院篆刻艺术委员会主任。

润笔价格：6000~8000/平尺
供收藏家参考

Fan Daniu is Vice President of Beikong Sky Academy of Traditional Chinese Painting, Director of Seal Carving Committee of China-Foreign Folk Art Exchange and Promotion Association, and Director of Seal Carving Committee of Beijing National Calligraphy and Painting Research Institute.

Reference price: RMB 6,000-8,000 per square feet

《黄河之水天上来》97*180　Yellow River Flowing Down From Heaven

冯训文 FENGXUNWEN

冯训文 1947年生，享受国务院政府特殊津帖，国家一级美术师，中国美术家协会会员，特聘为中华人民共和国外交部美术顾问。

润笔价格：25000~30000/平尺
供收藏家参考

Feng Xunwen, born in 1947, is a National Class A artist, receives Special Allowance of State Council of China, member of China Artists Association, and art consultant of Ministry of Foreign Affairs.

Reference price: RMB 25,000-30,000 per square feet

《墨汁一瓶酒一罇》 180*85 *A Bottle of Ink and A Glass of Liquor*

《山水》97*180　Mountain and River

胡振声
HU ZHENSHENG

胡振声，字叔镛，别署四正山人，现为中国书法家协会天津分会会员，中国京海书画艺术研究院副院长。

润格：8000~10000/平尺

供收藏家参考

Hu Zhensheng, with Shu Yong and Si Zheng Hermit as his literary names, is a member of Tianjin Branch of China Calligraphers Association and Vice President of China Jinghai Calligraphy and Painting Research Institute.

Reference price: RMB 8,000-10,000 per square feet

贾建国 JIA JIANGUO

贾建国 男，1955年，中国图书文化馆展览馆馆长，北京市美术家协会会员。

润笔价格：10000~15000/平尺
供收藏家参考

Jia Jianguo, born in 1955, is Curator of Exhibition Hall of China Book Culture Gallery and member of Beijing Artists Association.
Reference price: RMB 10,000-15,000 per square feet

《斜晖脉脉水悠悠》96*180 Setting Sun over Waterfalls

《定居》97*180　Settling Down

姜荣慧　男，祖籍山东蓬莱，黑龙江省美术家协会理事，黑河市美术家协会主席，黑河市书画院顾问。

润笔价格：13000~16000/平尺
供收藏家参考

姜荣慧
JIANG RONGHUI

Jiang Ronghui, with his ancestral home in Penglai, Shandong Province, is a council member of Heilongjiang Artists Association, President of Heihe Artists Association, and consultant of Heihe Calligraphy and Painting Gallery.

Reference price: RMB 13,000-16,000 per square feet

雷金池 LEI JINCHI

雷金池 河北徐水人,1940年11月生于天津静海县,河北省美术家协会常务理事,廊坊市美术家协会主席,国家一级美术师。

润笔价格:10000~15000/平尺
共收藏家参考、

《黄河之水天上来》180*97
Yellow River Flowing Down From Heaven

Lei Jinchi, born in Jinghai County, Tianjin, in November 1940 and with his ancestral home in Xushui, Hebei Province, is a standing council member of Hebei Artists Association and President of Langfang Artists Association. Lei is a National Class A artist.

Reference price: RMB 10,000-15,000 per square feet

李光华
LI GUANGHUA

李光华 1948年生于陕西岐山，师从西安美术学院教授，现就读中国艺术研究院中国美术创造院创研班，现任岐山书画院副院长。

润笔价格：8000~10000平尺
供收藏家参考

《云山秋韵》180*97　　Mountain in Autumn Mist

Li Guanghua, born in Xishan, Shaanxi Province, in 1948, graduated from Xi'an Academy of Fine Arts. As Vice President of Qishan Calligraphy and Painting Academy, Li is now studying in School of Chinese Fine Arts of Chinese National Academy of Arts.

Reference price: RMB 8,000-10,000 per square feet

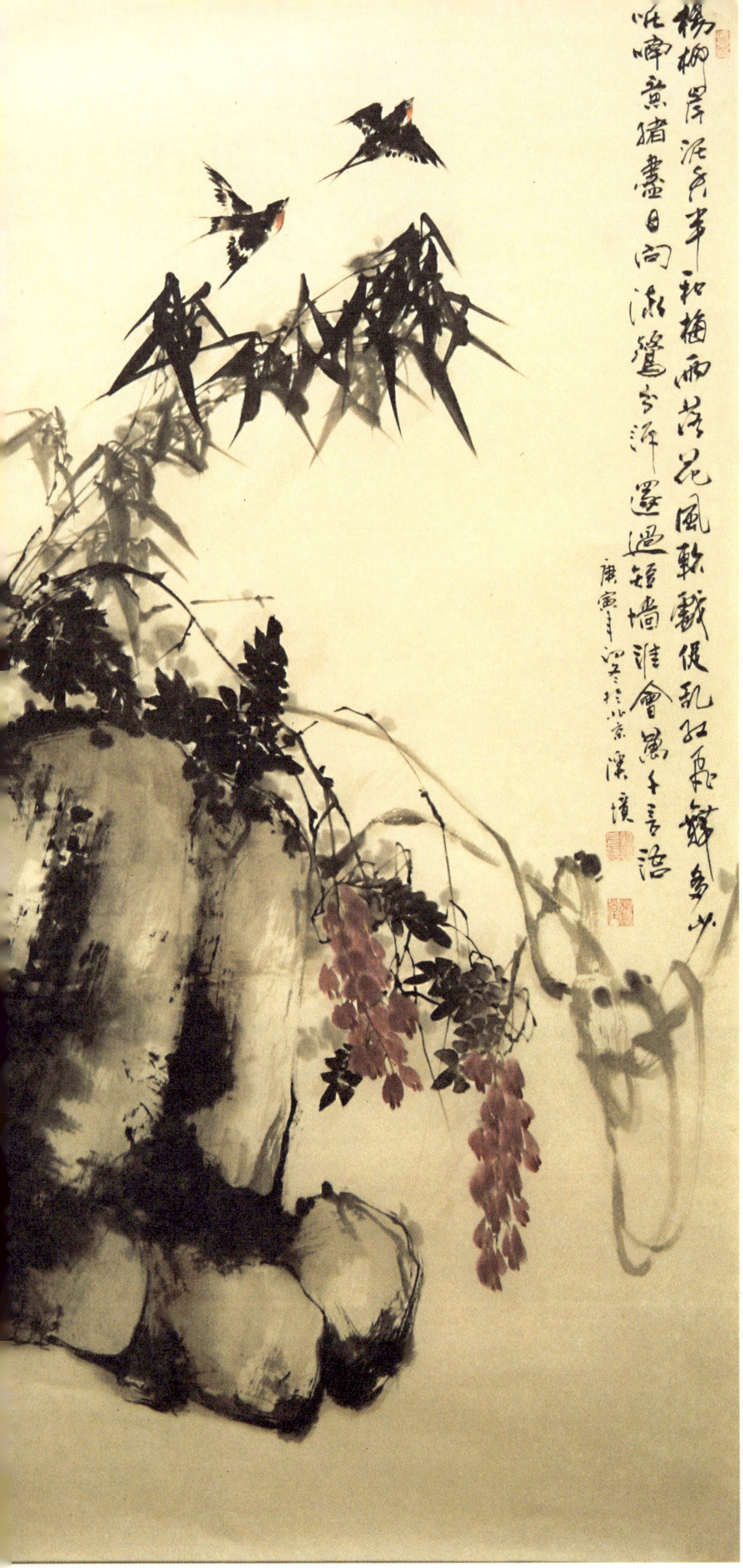

《花鸟》 *Flower and Birds*

李溪境 LI XIJING

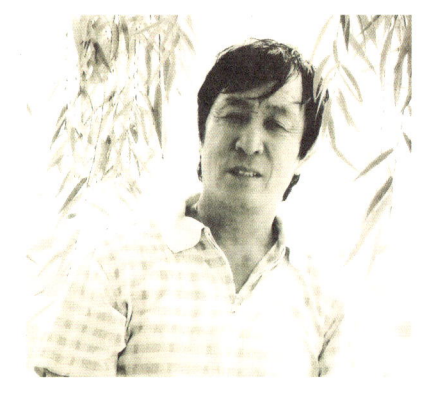

李溪境　中国美术家协会会员，国家一级美术师，中国美术家交流协会副秘书长，北京琉璃厂画院副院长。

润笔价格：12000~15000 平尺
供收藏家参考

Li Xijing is a member of China Artists Association, National Class A artist, Vice Secretary General of China Artists Communion Association, and Vice President of Beijing Liulichang Painting Gallery.

Reference price: RMB 12,000-15,000 per square feet

李振华 男，1974年生，中国青年美术家百杰，中国美术家协会河北分会会员。

润笔价格：5000~6000/平尺
供收藏家参考

Li Zhenhua, born in 1974, is among Top 100 Young Artists in China and member of Hebei Branch of China Artists Association.

Reference price: RMB 5,000-6,000 per square feet

《清闲一日睡至烟霞太行西》78*180 Dozing off till Sun Setting West of Mount Taihang

《啸天踏云》97*180 Singing over Clouds

刘长海 一九五五年出生，北京市美术家协会会员，北京湖社艺术研究会会员，丰台美术家协会理事，中国书法家协会会员。

润笔价格：6000~8000/平尺
供收藏家参考

Liu Changhai, born in 1955, is a member of Beijing Artists Association and of Beijing Hushe Art Research Institute, council member of Fengtai Artists Association, and member of China Calligraphers Association.

Reference price: RMB 6,000-8,000 per square feet

刘从善 LIU CONGSHAN

刘从善 生于1934年，北京华原翰墨书画院名誉院长，小学高级教师，界首市美协会员。

润笔价格：3000~5000/平尺
供收藏家参考

《相依》180*97　　Being Together

Liu Congshan, born in 1934, is a senior primary teacher, Honorary President of Beijing Huayuan Hanmo Painting Gallery, and member of Jieshou Artists Association.

Reference price: RMB 3,000-5,000 per square feet

莫松生 职业画家，一九七零年生，现为新民美术院分校中专国画工艺实训中心主任，中国国际书画艺术研究会会员，北京书画艺术交流中心业务部理事，广西书画协会会员。

润笔价格：5000~8000/平尺
供收藏家参考

莫松生
MO SONGSHENG

Mo Songsheng, born in 1970, is a professional painter. He is now Director of Traditional Chinese Painting and Crafts Training Center of Branch School of Xinmin Luxun Academy of Fine Arts, member of China International Association of Painting and Calligraphy, council member of Business Department of Beijing Calligraphy and Painting Art Exchanges Center, and member of Guangxi Calligrapher and Painter Association.

Reference price: RMB 5,000-8,000 per square feet

《漓江晨雾》100*250 *Lijiang River amid Morning Mist*

那士忠
NA SHIZHONG

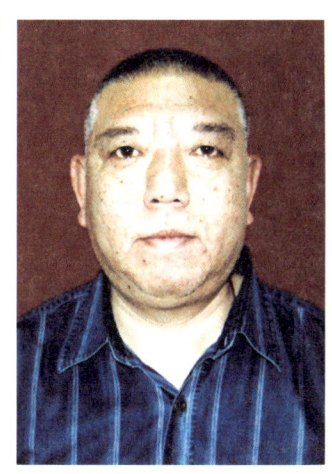

那士忠　现为哈尔滨市美术家协会会员、哈尔滨市书画研习绘画师、航空工业部美术协会会员、九州画院理事。

润笔价格：7000~9000/平尺
供收藏家参考

Na Shizhong, a Harbin-based painter, is a member of Harbin Artists Association, member of Artists Association under Ministry of Aviation Industry, and council member of Jiuzhou Painting Gallery.

Reference price: RMB 7,000-9,000 per square feet

《赏秋图》180*97　*Enjoying Autumn*

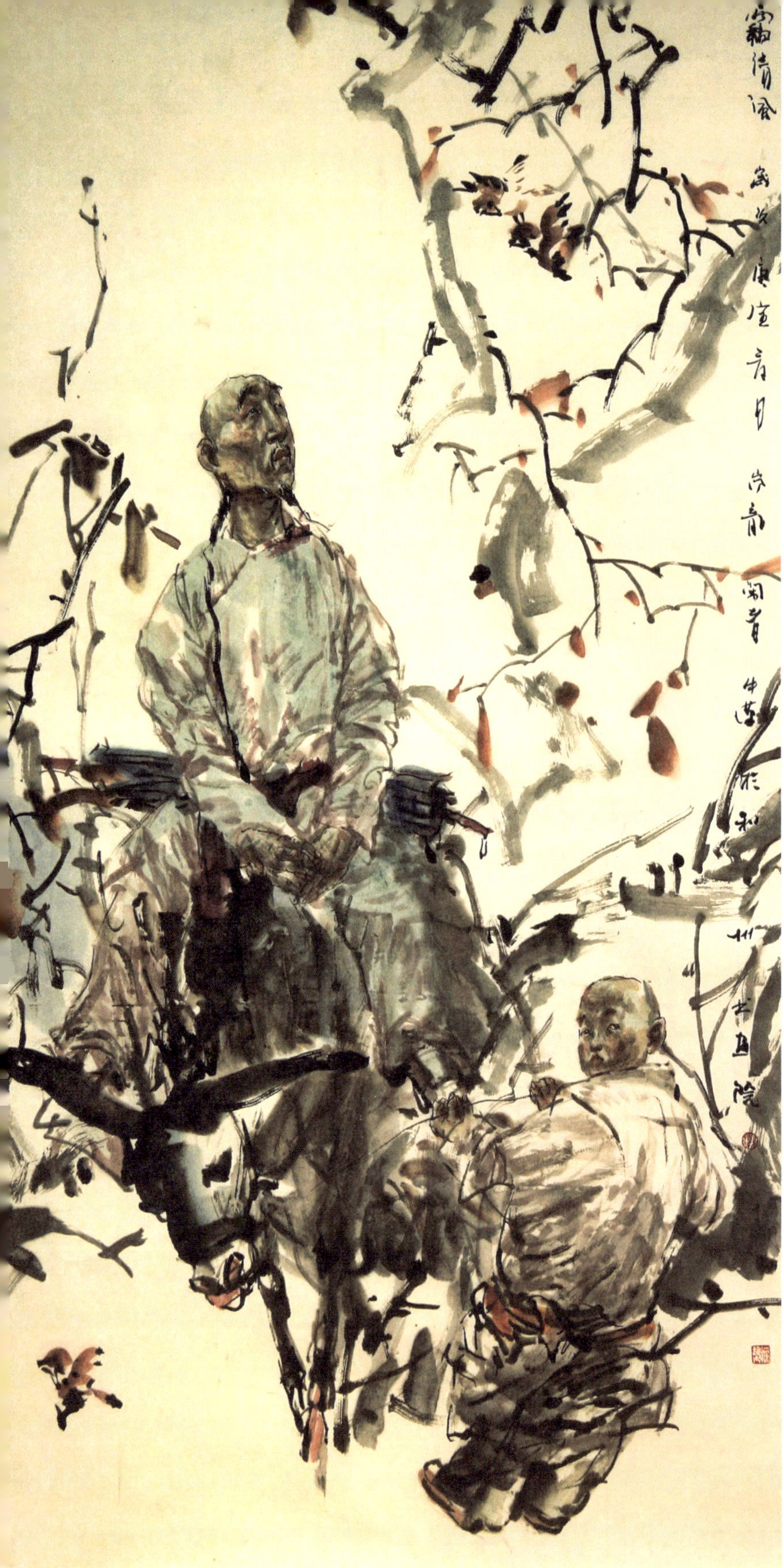

《两袖清风》180*97 *Righteousness and Uprightness*

牛 汉

NIU HAN

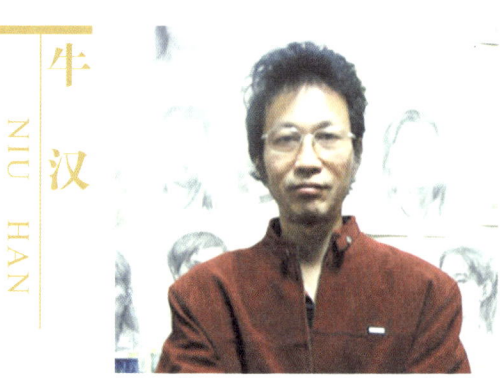

牛　汉　1957 年，回族，专职画家，安徽美协会员。

润笔价格：6000~9000/ 平尺
供收藏家参考

Niu Han, born in 1957 and of Hui nationality, is a professional painter and member of Anhui Artists Association.

Reference price: RMB 6,000-9,000 per square feet

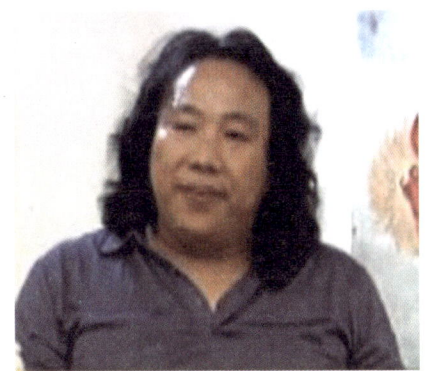

苏联瑞

苏联瑞 中国文联书画艺术交流中心创作员，国家人事部一级艺术委员，中国新闻国际出版社书画院理事。

润笔价格：3000~5000/平尺
供收藏家参考

Su Lianrui is a creative member of Center for Art Exchanges of China Federation of Literary and Art Circles, Class A member of Arts Committee of Ministry of Human Resources and Social Security, and council member of Calligraphy and Painting Gallery of China International News Press

Reference price: RMB 3,000-5,000 per square feet

《双雄》180*97　Two Roosters

中国当代书画名家作品收藏指南

苏新华 SU XINHUA

苏新华 1957年生,北京京海艺术研究院理事,河南省美协会员。

润笔价格:2000~3000/平尺
供收藏家参考

Su Xinhua, born in 1957, is a council member of Beijing Jinghai Art Research Institute and member of Henan Artists Association.

Reference price: RMB 2,000-3,000 per square feet

《觅踪》180*978 Tracking

陶善荣
TAO SHANRONG

陶善荣 别署石山，中国书画家协会理事，中国书画院名誉院长。

润笔价格：3000~5000/平尺
供收藏家参考

Tao Shanrong, with Shi Shan as his literary name, is a council member of China Calligrapher and Painter Association and Honorary President of China Painting and Calligraphy Academy

Reference price: RMB 3,000-5,000 per square feet

《莫道书圣爱其深》 *No Wonder Master Calligrapher Loved Its Deepness*

《明珠高挂玉液香》97*180 Bead-like Grapes and Fragrant Wine

王春生　男，1965年，汉族，燕南山书画院院长，中国画家协会会员，中国紫光阁名人书画院理事，一级美术师。

润笔价格：5000~6000/平尺

供收藏家参考

王春生
WANG CHUNSHENG

Wang Chunsheng, born in 1965 and of Han nationality, is President of Yannan Mountain Calligraphy and Painting Gallery, member of China Painters Association, council member of China Ziguang Pavilion Celebrity Calligraphy and Painting Gallery, and a Class A artist.

Reference price: RMB 5,000-6,000 per square feet

王福刚
WANG FUGAGN

王福刚 北京美协会员，一级美术师。

润笔价格：3000~4000/平尺
供收藏家参考

Wang Fugang is a member of Beijing Artists Association and a Class A artist.

Reference price: RMB 3,000-4,000 per square feet

《群鸟唱春曲》97*180 *Birds in Chorus to Announce Spring*

王根喜
WANG GENGXI

王根喜 字舟人，1954年生，河南南阳人，中国美术家协会河南分会会员，河南书画联谊会理事。

润笔价格：5000~8000/平尺
供收藏家参考

Wang Genxi, born in Nanyang, Henan Province, in 1954 and with Zhou Ren as his literary name, is a member of Henan Branch of China Artists Association and council member of Henan Calligrapher and Painter Federation.

Reference price: RMB 5,000-8,000 per square feet

《相伴紫晖》97*180 In Company with Purple Sunshine

王正春 1957年生于成都，现为中国书画艺术委员会会员，四川省美术家协会会员，四川绘画艺术院画师，成都市山水画会副秘书长。

润笔价格：6000~8000/平尺
供收藏家参考

《春满蜀山》180*97　*Mount Shushan in Spring*

Wang Zhengchun, born in Chengdu in 1957, is member of China Art Committee of Calligraphy and Painting, member of Sichuan Artists Association, painter with Sichuan Painting Academy, and Vice Secretary General of Chengdu Landscape Painting Society.

Reference price: RMB 6,000-8,000 per square feet

徐长有 XU CHANGYOU

徐长有 1938年生，四川美术家协会会员，中国石油画院一级画师，四川省水彩水粉画研究会会员。

润格：5000~8000/平尺

供收藏家参考

Xu Changyou, born in 1938, is a member of Sichuan Artists Association and Class A painter with China Petroleum Painting Gallery. Xu is also a member of Sichuan Watercolor and Gouache Painting Research Society.

Reference price: RMB 5,000-8,000 per square feet

《春雪出谷》180*97
Spring Snow in Valley

张 东
ZHANG DONG

张　东　男，1987年生，主要擅长画笑佛，职业画家。

润笔价格：3000~5000/平尺
供收藏家参考

《福大寿大》180*97 *Happiness and Longevity*

Zhang Dong, male and born in 1987, is a professional painter especially skilled in painting smiling Buddha.

Reference price: RMB 3,000-5,000 per square feet

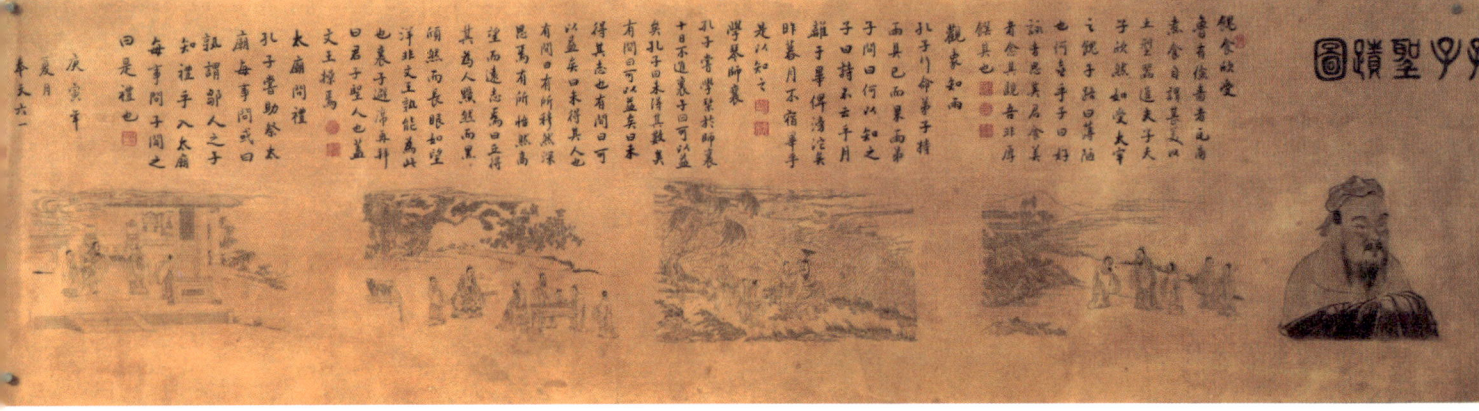

《孔子圣蹟图》36.5*173.5 Confucius' Traces

张光宇
ZHANG GUANGYU

张光宇 汉族，男，1965年生，中国书画研究院艺术委员会委员，中国当代艺术家协会培训中心荣誉教授，北京尔康书画院院士，陕西省诗书画研究会乾陵诗书画院副院长。

润笔价格：3000~5000/平尺
供收藏家参考

Zhang Guangyu, male, born in 1965, and of Han nationality, is a member of China Calligraphy and Painting Research Institute, honorary professor with Training Center of China Association of Contemporary Artists, painter with Beijing Erkang Painting Gallery, and Vice President of Qianling Poem, Calligraphy, and Painting Gallery of Shanxi Poem, Calligraphy and Painting Research Society.

Reference price: RMB 3,000-5,000 per square feet

张喜来 1957年，以画梅花为主，特钟情于冬梅。

润笔价格：3000~5000/平尺

供收藏家参考

张喜来
ZHANG XILAI

Zhang Xilai, born in 1957, is skilled in painting the plum blossom, especially the winter one.

Reference price: RMB 3,000-5,000 per square feet

《红梅》97*180 Red Plum Blossom

郑冰
ZHENG BING

郑 冰 1950年生于河南省开封市，中国美术家协会会员，河南省中国画研究院副院长，高级美术师，中国美协河南创作中心副主任，中国徐悲鸿画院国画艺委会山水画创作室副主任，中国新闻出版报社书画研究院副院长。

润笔价格：8000~10000/平尺
供收藏家参考

Zheng Bing, born in Kaifeng, Henan Province, in 1950, is a member of China Artists Association, Vice President and senior painter of Henan Institute of Chinese Painting, Vice Director of Henan Creation Center of China Artists Association, Vice Director of Landscape Painting Center under the Art Committee of Xu Beihong Gallery, and Vice President of Calligraphy and Painting Gallery of China International News Press.

Reference price: RMB 8,000-10,000 per square feet

《朱竹图》 97*180— Red Bamboos

周国亮
ZHOU GUOLIANG

周国亮　男，1957年生，擅长工笔人物。

润笔价格：3000~6000/平尺
供收藏家参考

Zhou Guoliang, male and born in 1957, is especially skilled in painting figures in the traditional Chinese realistic way.

Reference price: RMB 3,000-6,000 per square feet

《工笔观音》 *Avalokiteshvara*

扈照俊
HU ZHAOJUN

扈照俊 1946年生，河南商邱人，枣庄市美协和微湖书画研究会员，华厦诗文书画艺术家协会副秘书长，中国国画院鲁南分院院士。

润笔价格：3000~5000 平尺
供收藏家参考

Hu Zhaojun, born in Shangqiu, Henan Province, in 1946, is a member of Zaozhuang Artists Association and of Huihu Calligraphy and Painting Research Society, Vice President of Huaxia Association of Poetry, Calligraphy, and Painting, and member of Lunan Branch of China Institute of Traditional Chinese Painting.

Reference price: RMB 3,000-5,000 per square feet

《峡江风情》97*180 *A Sketch of Xiajiang*

《紫气东来》97*180 *Propitious Omen*

陈富宽
CHEN FUKUAN

陈富宽 男，1955年生于北京，北京师白艺术研究会常务理事，中国辛亥革命研究会书画理事，中共中央直属机关书画协会常务理事，北京齐白石艺术研究会常务理事，副秘书长，中国工艺美术学会会员，中国书画研究院西部创作院副院长。

润笔价格：8000~10000/平尺
供收藏家参考

Chen Fukuan, male, born in Beijing in 1955, is a standing council member of Beijing Shibai Art Research Society, calligraphy and painting council member of China 1911 Revolution Research Society, standing council member of Calligrapher and Painter Association of Organs Directly Under the Central Committee of the CPC, standing council member and Vice Secretary General of Beijing Qi Baishi Research Society, member of China Arts and Crafts Society, and Vice President of West China Creation Department of China Calligraphy and Painting Research Institute.

Reference price: RMB 8,000-10,000 per square feet

《云山云雾云中飞》97*180 *Flying Cloud over Mountains*

李宪润
LI XIANYUN

李宪润 字老成 号人东吾西，1936年生，滚笔山水、银粉水墨画创始者，著名画家，1956西安军校毕业，中国美术家协会青海分会秘书长，泰山书画院副院长，一级画师。

润笔价格：6000~8000/平尺
供收藏家参考

Li Xianru, born in 1936, is a famous painter. With Laocheng and Rendongwuxi as his literary names, he graduated from a military academy in 1956 and pioneered rolling-brush landscape painting and the use of aluminum powder in watercolor painting. He is a Class A artist, Secretary General of Qinghai Branch of China Artists Association and Vice President of Taishan Calligraphy and Painting Gallery.

Reference price: RMB 6,000-8,000 per square feet

刘清贵 LIU QINGGUI

刘清贵 1969年，中国画家村艺术顾问，江苏省美术家协会会员，江苏省书法家协会会员，西部书画艺术院副院长。

润笔价格：8000~10000/平尺
供收藏家参考

Liu Qinggui, born in 1969, is an art consultant of China Painter Village, member of Jiangsu Artists Association and of Jiangsu Calligraphers Association, and Vice President of West China Art Academy.

Reference price: RMB 8,000-10,000 per square feet

《秋月物语》 180*97
Story of Autumn

白启哲
BAI QIZHE

白启哲 北京市人,1935年出生,中国美术家协会会员,1991年 作品《黄山烟云》等20幅,在日本国千叶县举办"白雪石父子画展"。

润笔价格:35000~40000/平尺
供收藏家参考

Bai Qizhe, born in Beijing in 1935, is a member of China Artists Association. In 1991, he displayed 20 paintings including Mount Huangshan in Mist at Exhibition of Paintings of Bai Xueshi and His Son in Chiba Prefecture, Japan.

Reference price: RMB 35,000-40,000 per square feet

《峰峦叠嶂劲松青》
Peaks and Pines

王学文
WANG XUEWEN

王学文 1949年生，中国书画研究院艺术委员，中国书法家协会理事、一级美术师。

润笔价格：6000~7000/平尺
供收藏家参考

Wang Xuewen, born in 1949, is a Class A artist, council member of Art Committee of China Calligraphy and Painting Research Institute, and council member of China Calligraphers Association.

Reference price: RMB 6,000-7,000 per square feet

《西部黄土情》 180*97 *Love for Loess in West China*

《黄山飞瀑》68*206 *Waterfall at Mount Huangshan*

张文魁
ZHANG WENKUI

张文魁　1945年生，香港世界著名艺术家联合会会员，中国美术家协会会员北京美术家协会会员，中国书法家协会会员中国齐白石艺术研究会副会长，中国禅佛书画院副院长，北京古岸画院院长。

润笔价格：10000~15000/平尺
供收藏家参考

Zhang Wenkui, born in 1945, is a member of Hong Kong World Federation of Famous Artists, of Beijing Artists Association, of China Artists Association, and of China Calligraphers Association, Vice President of Qi Baishi Research Institute and of China Zen and Buddhist Painting Gallery, and President of Beijing Gu'an Painting Gallery.

Reference price: RMB 10,000-15,000 per square feet

张祖勇 ZHANG ZUYONG

张祖勇 字相勇 1967年生于浙江，先后就读于浙江工艺美校，中国画院画师，一级美术师。

润笔价格：8000~10000/平尺
供收藏家参考

Zhang Zuyong, born in Zhejiang in 1967 and with Xiangyong as his literary name, graduated from Zhejiang Arts and Crafts School. Zhang is now a Class A artist and painter with China Institute of Art Academy.

Reference price: RMB 8,000-10,000 per square feet

《湖山秋色》180*97 *Lake and Mountain in Autumn*

陈薪名
CHEN XINMING

陈薪名　1981年生，吉林省美术家协会会员，吉林市美术家协会会员，吉林北山画院画家。

润笔价格：5000~6000/平尺
供收藏家参考

Chen Xinming, born in 1981, is a member of Jilin Provincial Artists Association and of Jilin City Artists Association, and painter with Jilin Beishan Painting Gallery.

Reference price: RMB 5,000-6,000 per square feet

《秋水长天》180*97　*Autumn Water*

《瑞雪》53*230 Auspicious Snow

褚永光
CHU YONGGUAN

褚永光 1948年生，廊坊市群众艺术馆美术部主任，国家高级工艺美术师，中国书画艺术委员会委员。

润笔价格：5000~6000/平尺
供收藏家参考

Chu Yongguang, born in 1948, is Director of Fine Art Department of Langfang People's Gallery, a national senior crafts artist, and member of China Art Committee of Calligraphy and Painting.

Reference price: RMB 5,000-6,000 per square feet

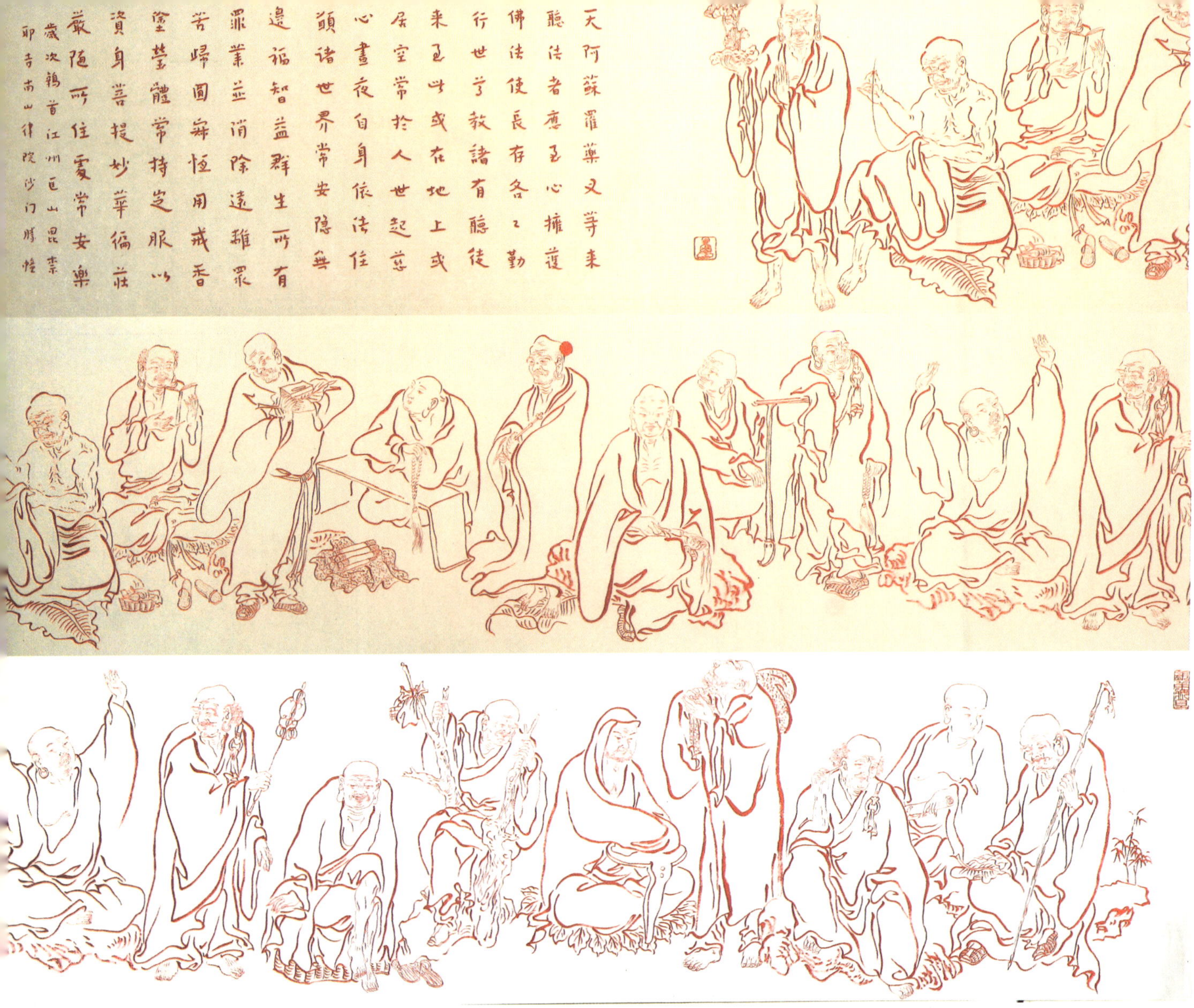

《罗汉造型》38*345 Arhats

邓金萍
DENG JINPING

邓金萍 1960年，女，职业画家。

润笔价格：2000~3000/平尺
供收藏家参考

Deng Jinping, born in 1960, is a professional painter.

Reference price: RMB 2,000-3,000 per square feet

龚　勇　号“野草山人”，汉族，福建省建瓯市人，三级美术师。“中国文化艺术发展促进会”会员，“金陵书画院”院士，“中国国画院”院士。

龚勇

GONG YONG

润笔价格：4000~5000/ 平尺
供收藏家参考

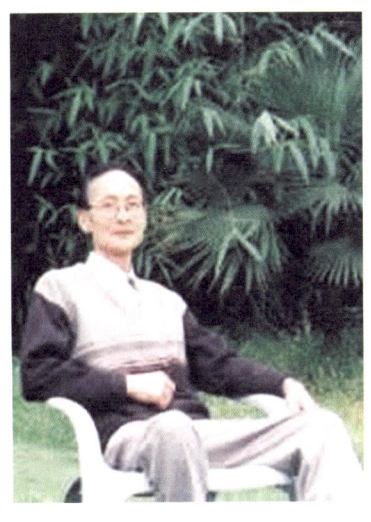

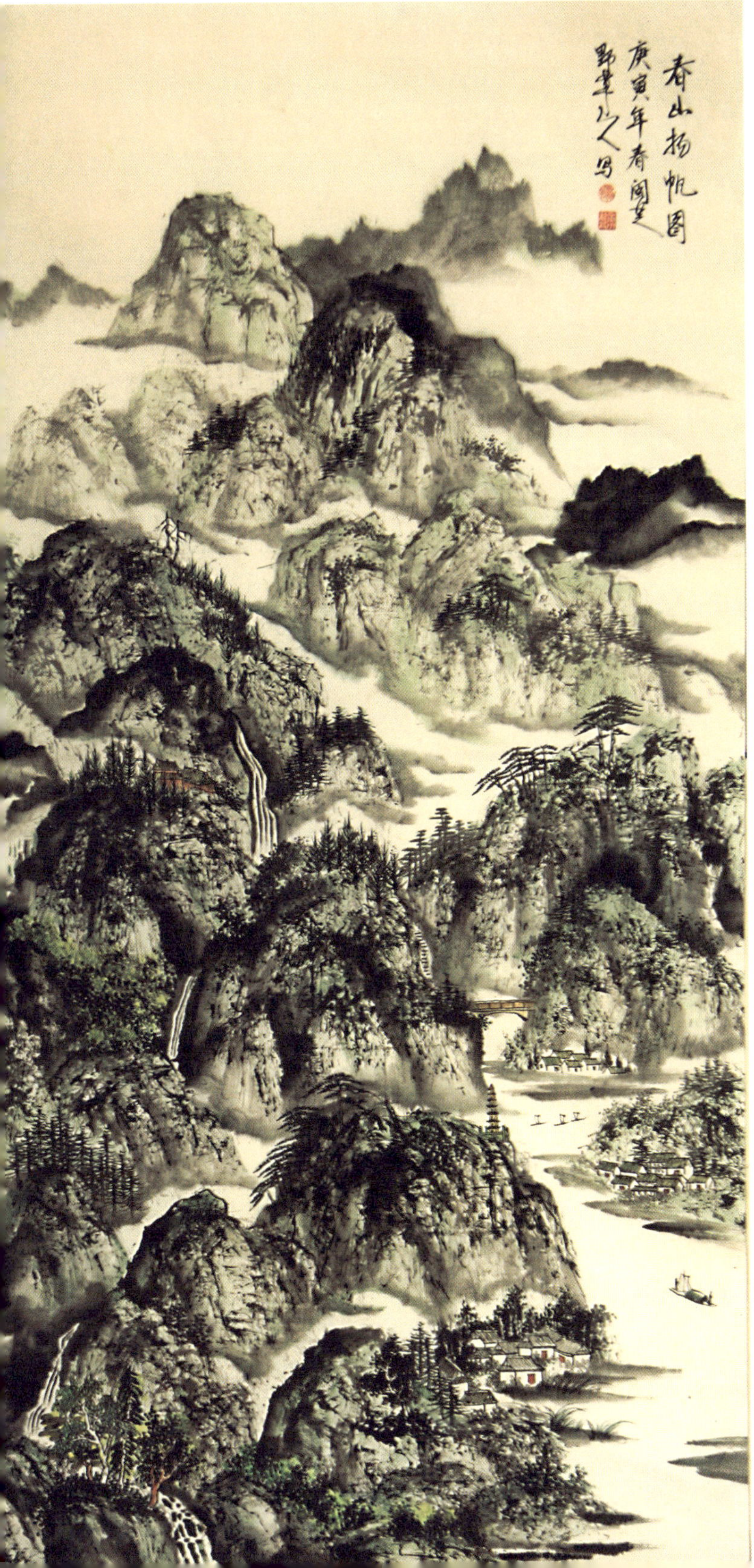

Gong Yong, born in Jian'ou, Fujian Province, and with Yecaoshanren as his literary name, is a Class C artist. He is a member of China Cultural and Art Promoting Society, and painter with Jinling Calligraphy and Painting Gallery and with China Traditional Chinese Painting Institute.

Reference price: RMB 4,000-5,000 per square feet

《春山扬帆图》

Sailing amid Mountains in Spring

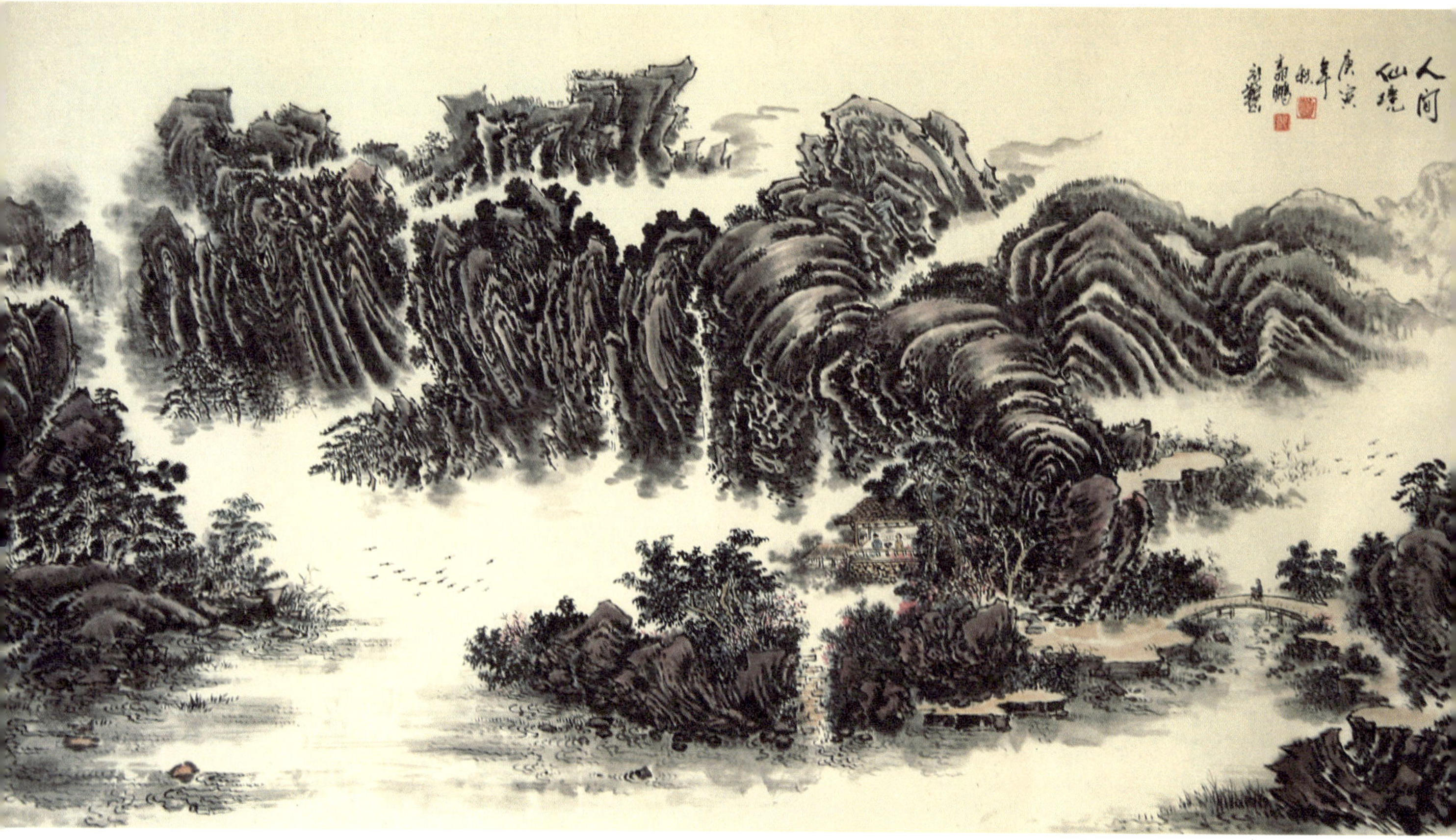

《人间仙境》97*180 *Paradise on Earth*

郭树鹏
GUO SHUPENG

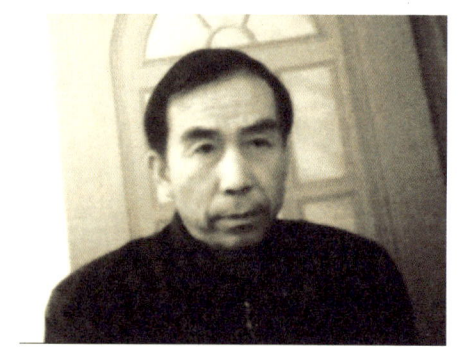

郭树鹏　男，1950年生，北京华夏国艺书画院院士，中国文人美术家协会会员，世界华人艺术联合会会员。

润笔价格：4000~5000/平尺
供收藏家参考

Guo Shuopeng, born in 1950, is a painter with Beijing Huaxia Guoyi Calligraphy and Painting Gallery, member of China Literary Artists Association, and member of WCNAA.

Reference price: RMB 4,000-5,000 per square feet

郭振霞
GUO ZHENXIA

郭振霞 男，1953年生，中国美术家协会河北邢台市会员。

润笔价格：3000~5000/平尺
供收藏家参考

Guo Zhenxia, born in 1953, is a member of Xingtai Branch of China Artists Association.

Reference price: RMB 3,000-5,000 per square feet

《观云瞻山》97*180　Viewing Clouds and Mountains

韩亚洲 HAN YAZHOU

韩亚洲 男，1941年生，中国美术家协会会员中国美术出版社编审。

润笔价格：18000~20000/平尺
供收藏家参考

Han Yazhou, born in 1941, is a member of China Artists Association and senior editor at China Fine Arts Publishing House.

Reference price: RMB18000-20000 per square feet

《对牛弹琴》97*180 *Playing Qin Facing A Bull 97*180*

《墨竹》97*180 Bamboos 97*180

郝冰川　北京云禅书画研究院书画家，中国书画研究院研究员，中国书画家学会会员，香港书画院一级画家，文化部诗书画院画家。

润笔价格：8000~9000/平尺
供收藏家参考

郝冰川
HAO BINGCHUAN

Hao Bingchuan is a calligrapher and painter with Beijing Yun Zen Calligraphy and Painting Research Institute, researcher with China Calligraphy and Painting Research Institute, member of China Calligrapher and Painter Association, Class A painter with Hong Kong Art Gallery, and painter with Calligraphy and Painting Gallery of the Ministry of Culture.

Reference price: RMB8000-9000 per square feet

侯贵喜
HOU GUIXI

侯贵喜 1968年生，中国书画印研究院高级研究员，香港东方文化中心馆员，一级美术师，《书画家》杂志社理事，专业画家等。

润笔价格：6000~8000/平尺
供收藏家参考

《二乔沐春图》 180*97 *Qiao Sisters in Spring* 180*97

Hou Guixi, born in 1968, is a senior research with Calligraphy, Painting and Seal Research Institute of China, librarian of Hong Kong Center of Oriental Culture, Class A artist, and council member and professional painter with magazine Calligraphy and Painting.

Reference price: RMB6000-8000 per square feet

《瓜果园》97*180 Orchard 97*180

冀希君
JI XIJUN

冀希君 1935年生于河北省枣强县，中国新疆美协会员，中国手指画研究会会员，中国书画家协会会员，中国美协网签约画家，中国艺术家协会会员。

润笔价格：8000~12000/平尺
供收藏家参考

Ji Xijun, born in Zaoqiang, Hebei Province, in 1935, is a member of Xinjiang Artists Association, of China Finger Painting Research Society, of China Calligrapher and Painter Association, of China Artist Association, and a contracted painter with CAAAN.

Reference price: RMB8000-12000 per square feet

陈宝勤 号汉南山樵，1959年9月生，中国书画研究院画家、导师，香港"国拍"特级画家，新加坡艺术协会常务理事，中国文人美协理事，中国书画家协会理事。

润笔价格：5000~6000/平尺
供收藏家参考

陈宝勤
CHEN BAOQIN

Chen Baoqin, born in September 1959 and with Hannanshanqiao as his literary name, is a painter and tutor with China Calligraphy and Painting Research Institute, special-grade painter with Hong Kong International Auction, standing council member of Singapore Art Society, council member of China Literary Artists Association, and council member of China Calligrapher and Painter Association.

Reference price: RMB5000-6000 per square feet

《云峰幽韵图》96*180
Quiet Peaks in Clouds 96*180

张汉武
ZHANG HANWU

张汉武　生于1954年，外交部书画协会副主席，多次获得中国美协金奖。

润格：5000~6000/平尺

供收藏家参考

Zhang Hanwu, born in 1954, is Vice President of Calligrapher and Painter Association of Foreign Ministry and a frequent winner of Gold Prize of China Artists Association.

Reference price: RMB5000-6000 per square feet

《高远图》　*Loftiness*

管 强
GUAN QIANG

管 强 1958年生，中国冰雪画研究会理事，中国长城画院画家，中国国家画院首届高研班毕业，黑龙江美协会员，黑龙江省画院特聘画家，一级美术师，牡丹江市冰雪画院副院长兼秘书长。

润笔价格：6000~8000/平尺
供收藏家参考

《杏花满枝又一春》96*180
Apricot Flowers in New Spring 96*180

Guan Qiang, born in 1958, is a council member of China Ice and Snow Painting Research Institute, painter with China Great Wall Painting Gallery. Among the first batch of graduates from the senior program in China National Academy of Painting, he is a member of Heilongjiang Artists Association, a specially employed painter of Heilongjiang Painting Gallery, Class A artist, and Vice President and Secretary General of Mudanjiang Ice and Snow Painting Gallery.

Reference price: RMB6000-8000 per square feet

《报春》96*180　Messenger of Spring　96*180

郭利杰
GUO LIJIE

郭利杰　中国书画家联谊会画家，陕西西北书画研究院副院长，陕西太白书画院名誉院长，陕西书画培训学院国画教授。

润笔价格：10000~15000/ 平尺
供收藏家参考

Guo Lijie is a painter with China Calligrapher and Painter Federation, Vice President of Northwest Calligraphy and Painting Research Institute, Honorary President of Taibai Calligraphy and Painting Research Institute in Shaanxi Province, and Traditional Chinese Painting Professor with Shaanxi Calligraphy and Painting Training College.

Reference price: RMB10000-15000 per square feet

李志刚
LI ZHIGANG

李志刚 中国美术家协会会员，潮州市美术家协会副主席，潮州师范学院艺术学院教授，中国画教研室主任。

润笔价格：10000~12000/平尺

供收藏家参考

《金玉满堂》180*97 Hall of Gold and Jade 180*97

Li Zhigang is a member of China Artists Association, Vice President of Chaozhou Artists Association, professor with School of Art and Director of Traditional Chinese Painting Teaching and Research Section in Chaozhou Normal College.

Reference price: RMB10000-12000 per square feet

《虾》97*180　　Shrimps 97*180

林玉华
LIN YUHUA

林玉华　1933年出生于福建莆田，高级画师、教授，中国国际书画艺术会研究员，中国老年书画研究会会员，新加坡神州艺术院高级顾问。

润笔价格：2000~4000/平尺
供收藏家参考

Lin Yuhua, born in Putian, Fujian Province, in 1933, is a senior painter and professor. Lin is a researcher of China International Research Institute of Calligraphy and Painting, member of China Calligraphy and Painting Research Institute for the Aged, and senior consultant of Singapore Shenzhou Art Gallery.

Reference price: RMB2000-4000 per square feet

王泽喜 山东省邹平县人，毕业于山东工艺美术学院，中国书画家协会理事，中国东方美术馆特聘画家。

润笔价格：8000~10000/平尺

供收藏家参考

王泽喜
WANG ZEXI

Wang Zexi, born in Zouping, Shandong Province, a graduate from Shandong College of Arts and Crafts, is a council member of China Calligrapher and Painting Association and painter with China Oriental Art Gallery.

Reference price: RMB8000-10000 per square feet

《荷塘清趣》 Lotus Pool

宋有基
SONG YOUJI

宋有基 现为大连市老年书画研究会会员，大连市书协会员，敦煌国际艺术研究会会员。

润笔价格：4000~6000/平尺
供收藏家参考

Song Youji is a member of Dalian Calligraphy and Painting Research Society for the Aged, of Dalian Calligraphers Association, and of Dunhuang International Art Research Society.

Reference price: RMB4000-6000 per square feet

《千秋盛世》96*180   *Perpetual Prosperity* 96*180

苏联春
SU LIANCHUN

苏联春 1971年生于北京，号"震风堂主"，荣滕四方书画社副社长，中原书画院高级画师，北京卢沟桥书画院画师，中华清风书画协会九洲书画院美术师。

润笔价格：20000~25000/平尺
供收藏家参考

《神威》97*180
Invincible Might 97*180

Su Lianchun, born in Beijing in 1971 and with Master of Zhenfeng Hall as his literary name, is Vice President of Rongteng Sifang Painting and Painting Studio, senior painter with Zhongyuan Calligraphy and Painting Gallery, Beijing Lugou Bridge Calligraphy and Painting Gallery, and Jiuzhou Calligraphy and Painting Gallery of China Qingfeng Calligrapher and Painter Association.

Reference price: RMB20000-25000 per square feet

孙春瑛
SUN CHUNYING

Family Union in Shade of Japanese Banana 96*180
《绿蕉阴下合家欢》96*180

孙春瑛 现为中艺卿云画院院士，北京东城书画协会会员，北京中国书画研究社办公室副主任，瓦屋画院副秘书长，华夏京都书画研究院研究员，中国山峡画院一级画师等。

润笔价格：3000~45000/平尺
供收藏家参考

Sun Chunying is a painter with Zhongyi Qingyun Painting Gallery, member of Dongcheng District Calligrapher and Painter Association in Beijing, Vice Director of China Calligraphy and Painting Research Society, Vice Secretary General of Wawu Painting Gallery, researcher with Huaxia Jingdu Calligraphy and Painting Research Institute, and Class A painter with China Shanxia Painting Gallery.

Reference price: RMB30000-45000 per square feet

《雄风》 *Awe-inspiring Bearing*

徐宝铭
XU BAOMING

徐宝铭 1944年生人，黑龙江省美术家协会会员，中国书画研究院研究员，中国田园画会常务理事，"八骏图"画马研究会副会长，绥化市文联副主席。

润笔价格：6000~7000/平尺
供收藏家参考

Xu Baoming, born in 1944, is a member of Heilongjiang Artists Association, researcher with China Calligraphy and Painting Research Institute, standing council member of China Pastoral Painting Society, Vice President of Horse Painting Research Society, and Vice President of Suihua Federation of Literary and Art Circles.

Reference price: RMB6000-7000 per square feet

张馨 ZHANG XIN

张 馨 张 鑫、张立昕、立新、墨儿得风堂主人，1966年生于河北省，早年随父习画，2005年就读于北京画院。

润笔价格：4000~5000/平尺
供收藏家参考

《晨风》 Morning Breeze

Born in Hebei Province in 1966, Zhang Xin, also known as Zhang Lixin and with Mo Er and Mistress of Dengfeng Hall as her literary name, learnt painting in her childhood from her father and studied in Beijing Painting Academy in 2005.

Reference price: RMB4000-5000 per square feet

王 敬
WANG JING

王　敬（艺名：梅湘子） 一级美术师，1964年生于广西桂林，现为中国书画家协会理事，世界艺术家协会副主席，中国书画家联谊会理事，中华当代艺术研究协会名誉会长，中国甲天下艺术集团创始总经理，华夏东方杰书画院常务理事。

润笔价格：10000~14000/平尺
供收藏家参考

Wang Jing, with Mei Xiangzi as his literary name, is a Class A artist. Born in Guangxi in 1964, he is a council member of China Calligrapher and Painter Association, Vice Chairman of World Artists Association, council member of China Calligrapher and Painter Federation, Honorary President of China Contemporary Art Research Association, founding General Manager of Jiatianxia Art Group, and standing council member of Huaxia Oriental Calligraphy and Painting Gallery.

Reference price: RMB10000-14000 per square feet

《群峰叠翠》 96*180 Green Peaks 96*180

王 钧 河北承德市人国家一级美术师，北京三百书画院画师。

润笔价格：6000~8000/平尺
供收藏家参考

王 钧
WANG YUN

Wang Jun, born in Chengde, is a National Class A artist and painter with Beijing 300 Calligraphy and Painting Gallery.

Reference price: RMB6000-8000 per square feet

《盼归图》96*180
Looking Forward to Return 96*180

《直挂云帆济沧海》 *Sailing Across Sea*

梁绿洲
LIANG LVZHOU

梁绿洲 1957年生，现为中国书画艺术院创作部副主任，中国美术家协会敦煌创作中心创作委员，国家一级美术师。

润笔价格：4000~5000/平尺
供收藏家参考

Liang Luzhou, born in 1957, is Vice Director of Creation Department of Chinese Painting and Calligraphy Art Academy, member of Dunhuang Creation Center of China Artists Association, and National Class A artist.

Reference price: RMB4000-5000 per square feet

王纪放
WANG JIFANG

王纪放 浙江人，1962年出生，现任中国书画艺术研究院副院长。

润笔价格：4000~5000/平尺
供收藏家参考

Wang Jifang, born in Zhejiang Province in 1962, is Vice President of China Calligraphy and Painting Art Institute for Research.

Reference price: RMB4000-5000 per square feet

《竹报平安》 Bamboo

徐振耀
XU ZHENYAO

徐振耀 1947年4月出生，中国艺术研究院创作委员，一级美术师，中国公关协会艺委会会员，国际美联艺术市场委员会理事。

润笔价格：4000~6000/平尺
供收藏家参考

Xu Zhenyao, born in April 1947, is a Class A artist, member of Chinese National Academy of Arts, member of Art Committee of China Public Relations Association, and council member of Art Market Committee of International Artists Association.

Reference price: RMB4000-6000 per square feet

《黄土高坡》180*97
Loess Plateau 180*97

杨汶千
YANG WEMQIAN

杨汶千 原名杨文乾，1966年5月出生，福建省漳州人，中国书法协会会员，中国书法艺术研究院常务理事，中国华侨文学艺术家协会理事。

润笔价格：6000~7000/平尺
供收藏家参考

Yang Wenqian, born in Zhangzhou, Fujian Province, in May 1966, is a member of China Calligraphers Association, standing council member of China Calligraphy Art Research Institute, and council member of China Association of Overseas Chinese Writers and Artists.

Reference price: RMB6000-7000 per square feet

《高枝已约风为有》96*180
Friendship between Branches and Wind 96*180

尹晓彦
YIN XIAOYANV

尹晓彦 笔名尹耐，1960年生，黑龙江巴彦人，北京中艺燕京书画院付院长，国家一级美术师。

润笔价格：5000~6000/平尺
供收藏家参考

《和谐幸福》 Harmony and Happiness

Yin Xiaoyan, with Yin Nai as his pen name, is a National Class A artist. Born in Baiyan, Heilongjiang Province, in 1960, he is Vice President of Beijing Zhongyi Yanjing Calligraphy and Painting Gallery.

Reference price: RMB5000-6000 per square feet

余展武
YU ZHANWU

余展武　又名东方烁，生于1945年，广东潮州饶平人，现为中国书画家协会理事。

润笔价格：2000~4000/平尺
供收藏家参考

Born in Chaozhou, Guangdong Province in 1945, Yu Zhanwu, also known as Dongfang Shuo, is a council member of China Calligrapher and Painter Association.

Reference price: RMB2000-4000 per square feet

《双松图》96*180
Picture of Twin Pines 96*180

李耀平
LI YAOPING

李耀平 男，1958年6月生，现为中央党校图书馆艺术顾问，美术教授，埃塞俄比亚大使馆书法师。中国水墨画研究院画家，文化部侨联文华阁书画院绘画艺委会委员。

润笔价格：8000~10000/平尺

供收藏家参考

Li Yaoping, born in June 1958, is now an arts consultant and Professor of Arts at Library of Party School of the Central Committee of CPC, calligrapher of Ethiopian Embassy, painter of China Research Institute of Ink and Wash Painting, and member of Arts Committee of Wenhua Pavilion Calligraphy and Painting Gallery of Overseas Chinese Federation under the Ministry of Culture.

Reference price: RMB8000-10000 per square feet

《森林里的水声》180*97
Sound of Water in Forest 180*97

刘辉煌
LIU HUIHUANG

刘辉煌 1941年生，祖籍江西萍乡，中国美术家协会会员，中国美术家协会插图装帧艺委会委员，中国出版工作者协会装帧艺术委员会副秘书长。

润笔价格：8000~10000/平尺
供收藏家参考

Liu Huihuang, born in 1941 and with his ancestral home in Pingxiang, Jiangxi Province, is a member of China Artists Association, member of Illustration and Design Committee of CAA, and Vice Secretary General of Illustration and Design Committee of Publishers Association of China.

Reference price: RMB8000-10000 per square feet

《高岭会友图》97*180 Meeting Friends 97*180

《万壑烟云》97*180   Cloud over Valleys 97*180

龙 云
LONG YUN

龙 云 女，1975年生，北京松云书画社秘书长

润笔价格：3000~5000/平尺
供收藏家参考

Long Yun, born in 1975, is Secretary General of Beijing Songyun Calligraphy and Painting Studio.
Reference price: RMB3000-5000 per square feet

《鱼花草》145*181 Fish, Flower and Grass 145*181

鲁　人　本名李春德，1930年出生于山东宁津，国家一级美术师，中国文联书画艺术交流中心创作员，国家人事部一级艺术委员，中国和合画院理事，中国新闻国际出版社书画院理事，中国书画家协会理事。

润笔价格：25000~30000/平尺
供收藏家参考

Lu Ren, literary name of Li Chunde, born in Ningjin, Shandong Province in 1930, is a National Class A artist. He is a creative member of Art Exchange Center of China Federation of Literary and Art Circles, Class A member of Arts Committee of Ministry of Human Resources and Social Security, council member of China Hehe Painting Gallery, council member of Calligraphy and Painting Gallery of China International News Press, and council member of China Calligrapher and Painter Association.

Reference price: RMB25000-30000 per square feet

《蓝牡丹寿鸟》97*180 Blue Peony and Longevity Birds 97*180

罗家宽
LUO JIAKUAN

罗家宽 1953年生于重庆，号云谷，三静堂主，现为中国残疾人美术家联谊会副会长，中国残疾人书画艺术中心主任。

润笔价格：6000~10000/平尺
供收藏家参考

Luo Jiakuan, born in Chongqing in 1953 and with Yungu and Master of Sanjing Hall, is Vice President of China Federation of Disabled Artists and Director of China Disabled Persons' Calligraphy and Painting Art Center.

Reference price: RMB6000-10000 per square feet

马双彦 MA SHUANGYAN

马双彦，1967年生，中国人文美术家协会会员、画家。

润笔价格：3000~4000/平尺
供收藏家参考

Ma Shuangyan, born in 1967, is a painter and member of China Humanities Artists Association.

Reference price: RMB3000-4000 per square feet

《上善若水》96*180 Water's Virtue 96*180

牧 野
MU YE

牧　野，男，原名殷维国，内蒙赤峰市人，山东省蓬莱市书画院院长，国家一级美术师，中国书画家协会理事。

润笔价格：15000~20000/平尺
供收藏家参考

MU YE, born in Chifeng, Inner Mongolia and previously known as Yin Weiguo, is Penghai Calligraphy and Painting Gallery in Shandong, National Class A artist, and council member of China Calligrapher and Painter Association.

Reference price: RMB15000-20000 per square feet

《草原骏马图》96*180　Horses in Prairie 96*180

牛 山 女，1961年生，湖南省美术家协会会员，东京书画院院士，中原书画院院士。

润笔价格：8000~10000/平尺
供收藏家参考

牛 山
NIU SHAN

Niu Shan, born in 1961, is a member of Hunan Artists Association, painter with Dongjing Calligraphy and Painting Gallery and with Zhongyuan Calligraphy and Painting Gallery.

Reference price: RMB8000-10000 per square feet

《白梅》180*97
White Plum Blossom 180*97

庞舜尧 又名庞亚，号听禅堂主人，恒一居士，1964年生于重庆市，现为中国书法家协会会员，北京中国画院花鸟部副主任。

润笔价格：3000~5000/平尺
供收藏家参考

庞舜尧 PANG SHUNYAO

Born in Chongqing in 1964, Pang Shunyao, also known as Pangya and with Master of Zen Hall and Hermit of Eternal One, is a member of China Calligraphers Association and Vice Director of Flower and Bird Painting Department of CIAA.

Reference price: RMB3000-5000 per square feet

《春讯》 Message of Spring

《七贤图》97*180 Seven Sages 97*180

钱 江
QIAN JIANG

钱 江 笔名潇竹,安徽省美术家协会会员,安徽省李鸿章研究会理事等。

润笔价格:3000~5000/平尺
供收藏家参考

Qian Jiang, with Xiaozhu as his literary name, is a member of Anhui Artists Association and council member of Anhui Li Hongzhang Research Society.

Reference price: RMB3000-5000 per square feet

任 嘉
REN JIA

《清泉碧水人欲醉》97*180　*Clean Spring and Green Water 97*180*

任　嘉　男，1944年生，永宁中学校长，中国书画研究院研究员，甘肃美协会员。

润笔价格：4000~5000/平尺
供收藏家参考

Ren Jia, born in 1944, is President of Yongning Middle School, researcher with China Calligraphy and Painting Research Institute, and member of Gansu Artists Association.

Reference price: RMB4000-5000 per square feet

田 诚
TIAN CHENG

《锦绣家园》97*180　Beautiful Home 97*180

田　诚（天成） 1960年出生于山东，中国美协敦煌创作中心创作委员，北京华夏诗联书画艺术研究院研究员，北京国画艺术家协会会员，北京中国画院画家。

润笔价格：3000~5000/平尺
供收藏家参考

Tian Cheng, born in Shandong Province in 1960, is a member of Dunhuang Creation Center of China Artists Association, researcher with Beijing Huaxia Shilian Calligraphy and Painting Research Institute, member of Beijing Traditional Chinese Painters Association, and painter with CIAA.

Reference price: RMB3000-5000 per square feet

中国当代书画名家作品收藏指南

宋繁林
SONG FANLIN

宋繁林 生于山东济南,现为中国和韵文化产业传媒机构副董事长,中国书画艺术研究院执行院长。

润笔价格:4000~5000/平尺
供收藏家参考

Song Fanlin, born in Jinan, Shandong Province, is Vice President of China Heyun Culture Industry Media Framework Co., Ltd and executive President of China Calligraphy and Painting Institute for Research.

Reference price: RMB3000-5000 per square feet

《秋山流泉》
Flowing Spring in Autumn Mountain

王翰尊 WANG HANZUN

王翰尊 汉族，1954年10月27日生于北京，翰尊艺术创作室主持人，中国美术艺术家协会会员，中国书法家协会会员。

润笔价格：10000~15000/平尺
供收藏家参考

Wang Hanzu, of Han nationality and born in Beijing on October 27th, 1954, is President of Hanzun Art Studio, member of China Artists Association and of China Calligraphers Association.

Reference price: RMB10000-15000 per square feet

《南无智慧胜佛》 Wisdom Buddha

《富贵春常在》 97*180　　Eternal Wealth and Spring 97*180

王怀清
WANG HUAIQING

王怀清　1963年8月14日出生于四川省眉山，四川省美术家协会会员，中国书画家联谊会会员，中国农民书画研究会创作员，眉山市美术家协会会员。

润笔价格：15000~20000/平尺
供收藏家参考

Wang Huaiqing, born in Meishan, Sichuan Province, on August 14th, 1963, is a member of Sichuan Artists Association and of China Calligrapher and Painter Federation, creative member of China Peasant's Calligraphy and Painting Research Association, and member of Meishan Artists Association.

Reference price: RMB15000-20000 per square feet

辛晋瑛　1932年生，中国工艺美术学会会员，原石家庄书画院名誉院长。

润笔价格：8000~10000/平尺
供收藏家参考

《雪幔古刹》93*174
Ancient Temple in Winter 93*174

辛晋瑛
XIN JINYING

Xin Jinying, born in 1932, is a member of China Arts and Crafts Society and former Honorary President of Shijiazhuang Calligraphy and Painting Gallery

Reference price: RMB8000-10000 per square feet

杨启运
YANG QIYUN

杨启运 男，1948年生，陕西省老年书画学会会员。

润笔价格：2000~3000/平尺
供收藏家参考

Yang Qiyun, born in 1948, is a member of Shaanxi Senior Citizens' Calligraphy and Painting Society.

Reference price: RMB2000-3000 per square feet

《皇帝手植柏》 180*97
Cypress Planted by Emperor 180*97

尹茂舟
YIN MAOZHOU

尹茂舟 1936年生，中国书画家协会会员，中国文化艺术发展促进会会员，中华当代名人书画研究会会员。

润笔价格：2000~3000/平尺
供收藏家参考

Yin Maozhou, born in 1936, is a member of China Calligrapher and Painter Association, of China Cultural and Art Promoting Society, and of China Research Society of Contemporary Famous Calligraphers and Painters.

Reference price: RMB2000-3000 per square feet

《峡江金秋》97*180　*Xiajiang in Golden Autumn*　97*180

尹钟骐 YIN ZHOUQI

尹钟骐 男，1955年11月25日出生，安徽省书法家协会会员，湖南省美术馆特聘画师。

润笔价格：4000~5000/平尺
供收藏家参考

《青山暮韵》 *Green Mountain at Sunset*

Yin Zhouqi, born on November 25th, 1955, is a member of Anhui Calligraphers Association and painter with Hunan Art Gallery.

Reference price: RMB4000-5000 per square feet

张春海
ZHANG CHUNHAI

张春海 回族 1964 年生，黑龙江省美术家协会会员，齐齐哈尔美术家协会会员，齐齐哈尔中国画研究院理事。

润笔价格：5000~8000/ 平尺
供收藏家参考

Zhang Chunhai, of Hui nationality and born in 1964, is a member of Heilongjiang Artists Association, of Qiqihar Artists Association, and council member of Qiqihar Traditional Chinese Painting Research Institute.

Reference price: RMB5000-8000 per square feet

《野蒲碧月》97*180   *Wild Calamus and Moon 97*180*

张满仓
ZHANG MANCANG

张满仓 1948年生于北京，中国书法研究院一级画师。

润笔价格：7000~8000/平尺
供收藏家参考

Zhang Mancang, born in Beijing in 1948, is a Class A painter with China Calligraphy Research Institute.

Reference price: RMB7000-8000 per square feet

《龟兹之舞》190*95　Qiuci Dance 190*95

《松花酿酒 春水煎茶》68*137　　Making Liquor with Pine Pollen and Tea with Spring Water 68*137

张子建
ZHANG ZIJIAN

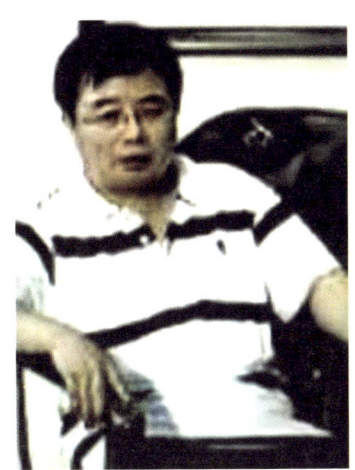

张子建　（张建华）1970 年生，河北无极人，1995 年毕业于河北师范大学美术系，现执教于石家庄学院美术系，从事中国画的教学、创作与研究。

润笔价格：8000~10000/ 平尺

供 收 藏 家 参 考

Zhang Zijian (also known as Zhang Jianhua), born in 1970, is a native of Wuji, Hebei Province. In 1995, he graduated from Department of Fine Arts of Hebei Normal University and is now a teacher in Department of Fine Arts of Shijiazhuang College, teaching, creating, and researching traditional Chinese painting.

Reference price: RMB8000-10000 per square feet

周恩高 ZHOU ENGAO

周恩高 1947年出生于湖北，湖北省美术家协会会员，恩施土家族苗族自治州美协副主席，湖北楚天画院院士，中原书画研究院客座教授。

润笔价格：6000~8000/平尺

供收藏家参考

Tujia Style 《土家天风》

Zhou Engao, born in Hubei Province in 1947, is a member of Hubei Artists Association, Vice President of Enshi Artists Association, painter with Hubei Chutian Painting Gallery, and visiting professor with Zhongyuan Calligraphy and Painting Research Institute.

Reference price: RMB6000-8000 per square feet

朱淑玉
ZHU SHUYU

朱淑玉 女，1963年生，中国文联书画艺术交流中心一级创作文员，四川省美术家协会会员，眉山市美术家协会会员。

润笔价格：10000~15000/平尺
供收藏家参考

Zhu Shuyu, born in 1963, is a Class A creative member of Center for Art Exchanges of China Federation of Literary and Art Circles, member of Sichuan Artists Association and of Meishan Artists Association.

Reference price: RMB10000-15000 per square feet

《锦绣前程》 97*180   Bright Prospects 97*180

中国当代书画名家作品收藏指南

黄毕济
HUANG BIJI

黄毕济 1936年1月生，师从姚治华，卢汉华，黄孙祝等名家，自成一格，作品曾入选获奖各类书画大展，入编多部书画典籍。

润笔价格：6000~8000/平尺

供收藏家参考

《霜叶红于二月花》 178*96　Red Maples　178*96

Huang Biji, born in January 1936, is a student of Masters Yao Zhihua, Lu Hanhua, and Huang Sunzhu. His works have frequently won prizes and been included in books on calligraphy and painting.

Reference price: RMB6000-8000 per square feet

李 铁
LI TIE

李 铁　1958年生，擅长写意花鸟，专业画家。

润笔价格：4000~5000/平尺
供收藏家参考

Li Tie, born in 1958, is a professional painter, especially skilled at bird-and-flower painting in liberal style.

Reference price: RMB4000-5000 per square feet

《铁骨生辉》96*180　*Red Plum Blossom 96*180*

理习忠 祖籍河南西华，北京金大都画院副院长，北京万博画院艺术顾问，一级画师。

润笔价格：8000~12000/平尺

供收藏家参考

理习忠
LI XIZHONG

Xi Lizhong, with his ancestral home in Xihua, Henan Province, is Vice President of Beijing Jindadu Calligraphy and Painting Gallery, art consultant and Class A painter with Beijing Wanbo Painting Gallery.

Reference price: RMB8000-12000 per square feet

《山野牧归图》 97*180 *Returning from Pasture 97*180*

刘萱林
LIU XUANLIN

刘萱林 男，1933年生，现为中国美术家协会安徽会员，国家高级工艺美术师。

润笔价格：5000~6000/平尺
供收藏家参考

《松龄鹤寿》180*97
Pine and Crane 180*97

Liu Xuanlin, born in 1933, is a member of Anhui Branch of China Artists Association, and a National Senior Artist.

Reference price: RMB5000-6000 per square feet
供收藏家参考

刘振江
LIU ZHENJIANG

刘振江 男,汉族,1952年1月生,山东滨县人,中国书法家协会会员,中国美术家协会北京分会会员,北京书法家协会会员。

润笔价格:6000~8000/平尺
供收藏家参考

Liu Zhenjiang, of Han nationality and born in Bin County, Shandong Province in January 1952, is a member of China Calligraphers Association, of Beijing Branch of China Artists Association, and of Beijing Calligraphers Association.

Reference price: RMB6000-8000 per square feet

《春山烟云入画屏》67*137 Mountain Mist in Spring 67*137

《空幽》97*180 Void 97*180

鲁 闽 | LU MIN

鲁 闽 1959年10月生,祖籍山东,现为清华大学美术学院教授。

润笔价格:15000~20000/平尺
供收藏家参考

Lu Min, born in October 1959 and with his ancestral home in Shandong, is a professor with Academy of Arts and Design, Tsinghua University.

Reference price: RMB15000-20000 per square feet

《太行秋韵》 97*180 *Mount Taihang in Autumn* 97*180

骆 云
LUO YUN

骆 云 中国美协河北分会会员，河北山水画研究会理事，国家奥林匹克书画大赛特聘画家。

润笔价格：8000~12000/平尺
供收藏家参考

Luo Yun is a member of Hebei Branch of China Artists Association, council member of Hebei Landscape Painting Research Institute, and painter with National Olympic Calligraphy and Painting Contest.

Reference price: RMB8000-12000 per square feet

孟 清
MENG QING

孟 清 湖北，女，1969年生，现为中华妇女书画家联谊会会员，咸宁市美术家协会副秘书长，第八届通山县政协委员。

润笔价格：6000~8000/平尺

供收藏家参考

Meng Qiang, born in Hubei Province in 1969, is a member of China Women Calligrapher and Painter Federation, Vice Secretary General of Xianning Artists Association, and member of the 8th CPPCC of Tongshan County.

Reference price: RMB6000-8000 per square feet

《杜鹃花放满枝春》180*100 *Rhododendron 180*100*

方本幼
FANG BENYOU

方本幼 字鹤来，绍兴人，中国美术学院中国画专业毕业，现为中国国家画院研究员。

润笔价格：15000~20000/平尺

供收藏家参考

Fang Benyou, with Helai as his literary name, is a native of Shaoxing. A graduate from Department of Traditional Chinese Painting of China Academy of Fine Arts, he is a researcher with China National Academy of Painting.

Reference price: RMB15000-20000 per square feet

《黄岳烟云》97*180　Cloud in Mount Huangshan 97*180

《任重道远》67*137　　*A Long Way 67*137*

宋连启 SONG LIANQI

宋连启　字松奇，52年9月出生，现为中国美协北京会员，中国书画家职工联谊会理事。

润笔价格：10000~12000/平尺
供收藏家参考

Song Lianqi, with Songqi as his literary name and born in September 1952, is a member of Beijing Branch of China Artists Association and council member of China Calligraphy and Painting Staff Federation.

Reference price: RMB10000-12000 per square feet

《盗仙草》 Stealing Herbal Cure-all

王春秋
WANG CHUNQIU

王春秋 又名炅秦、自号邀月草堂主人，现为联合国教科文卫组织专家组成员（亚洲区）、中国书法美术家协会会员、中国国画院创作委员会副主席、河北省美术家协会会员。

润笔价格：4000~5000/平尺
供收藏家参考

WangChunQiu, another name wishes from number qin, invited month for the United Nations, is now harmonica university master of education organization expert group (Asia), Chinese calligraphy artist association member, China academy of creation the vice chairman of the committee, hebei province artist association member.

Reference price: RMB4000-5000 per square feet

王德法
WANG DEFA

王德法 男，生于1968年，毕业于天津美术学院，现为河北美术家协会会员。

润笔价格：8000~10000/平尺
供收藏家参考

Wang Defa, born in 1968, is a graduate from Tianjin Academy of Fine Arts and member of Hebei Artists Association.

Reference price: RMB8000-10000 per square feet

《一片秋云一点霞》

A Piece of Autumn Cloud and A Spot of Red Cloud

王立文
WANG LIWEN

王立文 1940年9月生,河南温县人,军旅画家,国际中国书画家交流促进会艺委会秘书长。曾参与组织多次全国书画大展。任画册主编、艺术顾问等职。

润笔价格：6000~8000/平尺
供收藏家参考

Wang Liwen, born in Wen County, Henan Province in September 1940, is a military painter and Secretary General of Arts Committee of International Exchanges and Promotion Association of Chinese Calligraphers and Painters. He had participated in organization of many national exhibitions of calligraphy and painting. He also serves as editor in chief of pictorials and art consultant.

Reference price: RMB6000-8000 per square feet

《富贵平安》180*97　Wealth and Peace 180*97

王志鸿
WANG ZHIHONG

王志鸿 北京市人，著名花鸟画家王静如先生之长女，中国国画家协会理事，国际书画艺术研究会会员，北京齐白石艺术研究会理事，中华人民共和国大典编委委员，国家二级美术师。

润笔价格：3000~4000/平尺
供收藏家参考

Wang Zhihong, born in Beijing, is the eldest daughter of Wang Jingchu, a famous bird-and-flower painter. She is a council member of China Traditional Chinese Painters Association, member of International Association of Painting and Calligraphy, council member of Qi Baishi Research Institute, compiler of Grand Book of PRC, and National Class B artist.

Reference price: RMB3000-4000 per square feet

《春风暖翠》 96*180
Warm and Green Spring 96*180

邬杰民 WU JIEMIN

邬杰民 1958年生于北京，又名云鹤，中国艺术研究院研究中心专职画家，曾获"首都青年画家十杰"美誉。

润笔价格：15000~20000/平尺
供收藏家参考

《映日春晖》180*96 *Warm and Green Spring 180*96*

Wang Zhihong, born in Beijing, is the eldest daughter of Wang Jingchu, a famous bird-and-flower painter. She is a council member of China Traditional Chinese Painters Association, member of International Association of Painting and Calligraphy, council member of Qi Baishi Research Institute, compiler of Grand Book of PRC, and National Class B artist.

Reference price: RMB3000-4000 per square feet

傅振明　国家一级美术师，中央书画院院士，中国美术家协会会员，中国文化艺术国际交流中心艺委会常务理事，世界美术家联合艺术委员会委员，中国工艺美术家协会会员。

润笔价格：5000~6000/平尺
供收藏家参考

傅 振 明
FU ZHENMING

《日暮山风吹雨去》 *Evening in Mountain*

Fu Zhenming is a National Class A artist, painter with Central Calligraphy and Painting Institute, member of China Artists Association, standing council member of China International Culture and Art Exhibition Center, member of Arts Committee of World Artists Federation, and member of CACAA.

Reference price: RMB5000-6000 per square feet

汪 斌
WANG BIN

汪　斌　字佃斌，1960年生，国家一级画师，中国书画艺术研究院齐鲁分院副院长，万祥陶瓷协会会长，艺海阁书画室经理。

润笔价格：5000~6000/平尺
供收藏家参考

Wang Bin, with Dianbin as his literary name, born in 1960, is a National Class A painter, Vice President of Qilu Branch of China Calligraphy and Painting Research Institute, President of Wanxiang Porcelain Association, and Manager of Yihaige Calligraphy and Painting Studio.

Reference price: RMB5000-6000 per square feet

《云山秋韵》Mountain in Autumn Mist

袁胜聪
YUAN SHENGCONG

袁胜聪 男，1954年12月生，广西美协会员，中国美术家协会会员，中国书画家协会会员，中国画家协会理事，中原书画院高级书画师。

润笔价格：4000~6000/平尺
供收藏家参考

Yuan Shengcong, born in December 1954, is a member of Guangxi Artists Association, of China Artists Association, of China Calligrapher and Painter Association, council member of China Painters Association, and senior calligrapher with Zhongyuan Calligraphy and Painting Gallery.

Reference price: RMB4000-6000 per square feet

《明仕奇峰》 180*97
Peaks 180*97

《鸭戏荷塘》97*180　Ducks in Lotus Pond 97*180

张大川
ZHANG DACHUAN

张大川　现任王羲之国际书画院院长，中华人民共和国人事部，中国人才研究会艺术家学部委员会，国家一级艺术委员。

润笔价格：6000~8000/平尺
供收藏家参考

Zhang Dachuan is President of Wang Xizhi International Calligraphy and Painting Gallery, member of Artists Committee of China Talents Society, and National Class A art commissioner.

Reference price: RMB6000-8000 per square feet

《九秋风露鹤精神》97*180　　*Sprit of Crane* 97*180

赵文波　1963年生，黑龙江美协会员，齐齐哈尔市书协。

润笔价格：4000~5000/平尺
供收藏家参考

Zhao Wenbo, born in 1963, is a member of Heilongjiang Artists Association and of Qiqihar Calligraphers Association.

Reference price: RMB4000-5000 per square feet

《青山依旧在》97*180　*Green Mountains Stay 97*180*

朱元斋
ZHU YUANZHAI

朱元斋　1943年出生于临川，当他以娴熟的喷漆技术将调好的颜料喷射上画板，果然产生了想不到的奇妙效果，色泽光洁均匀，底色形象逼真。

润笔价格：3000~4000/平尺
供收藏家参考

Zhu Yuanzhai, born in Linchuan in 1943, created unimaginably spectacular effects when he skillfully sprayed well mixed paints at the drawing board: smooth and even colors and a vivid background.

Reference price: RMB3000-4000 per square feet

马远东
MA YUANDONG

马远东 1957年生于北京，北京美术家协会会员，中国书法艺术研究院艺术委员会会员。

润笔价格：5000~6000/平尺
供收藏家参考

Ma Yuandong, born in Beijing in 1957, is a member of Beijing Artists Association and of Arts Committee of China Calligraphy Research Institute.

Reference price: RMB5000-6000 per square feet

《天边有一群羊》96*180 *A Flock of Sheep at the Horizon* 96*180

李大成
LI DACHENG

《红枫树下谁为伴》 200*200   Company in the Shade of Red Maples 200*200

李大成 1966年10月生于福建，中国美术家协会会员，中国工笔画学会理事，现代工笔画院画家，解放军上海政治学院副教授。

润笔价格：20000~35000/平尺
供收藏家参考

Li Dacheng, born in Fujian Province in October 1966, is a member of China Artists Association, council member of China Hue Art Society, painter with Art Academy of Meticulous Painting, and assistant professor with Shanghai Branch of PLA Nanjing Institute of Politics.

Reference price: RMB20000-35000 per square feet

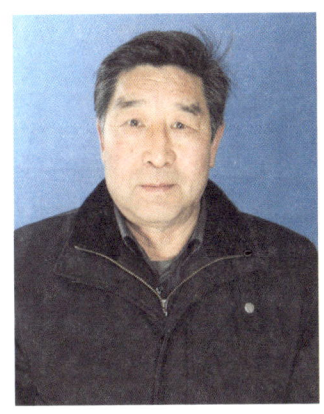

郭守勤
GUO SHOUQIN

郭守勤 1948年生，徽县公安局政委，积极参加举办的书画大赛多次获奖。

润笔价格：3000~5000/平尺
供收藏家参考

《秦岭人家》180*97
A Household at Qinling Mountains 180*97

Guo Shouqin, born in 1948, is Political Commissar of Hui County Bureau of Public Security. Often participating in calligraphy and painting contests, he has won many prizes.

Reference price: RMB3000-5000 per square feet

王金奎
WANG JINKUI

王金奎 男,1947年生,现任中国国家友好画院,中国汉唐画院,世界著名艺术家协会会员,中国拍卖企业联盟终生荣誉顾问。

润格:5000~6000/平尺
供收藏家参考

Wang Jinkui, born in 1947, is a member of National Friendship Painting Academy, of Hantang Paining Gallery, and of World Association of Famous Artists, and life-tenured honorary consultant of China Auction Industry Union.

Reference price: RMB5000-6000 per square feet

《玉龙雪瑞金沙图》180*96
Yulong Snow Mountain 180*96

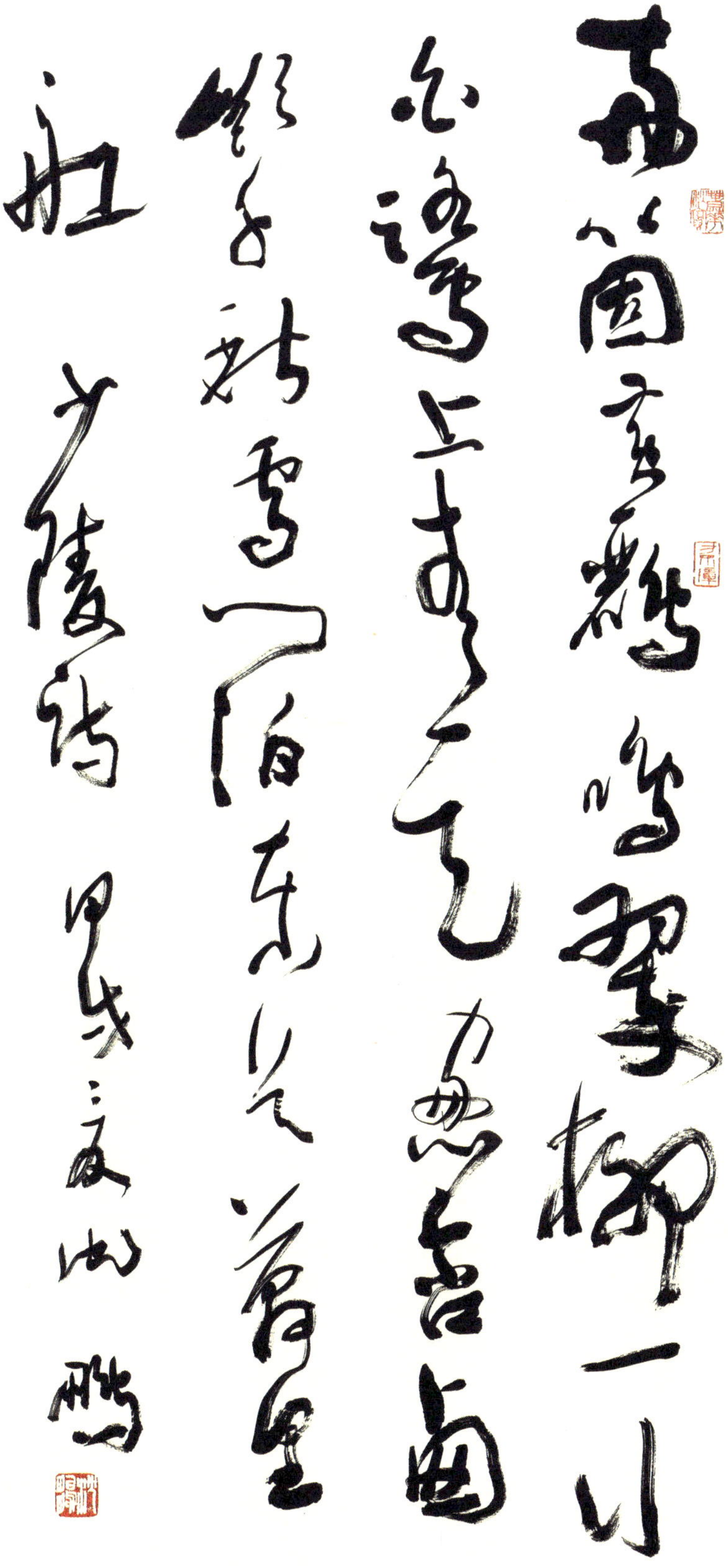

沈 鹏
SHEN PENG

沈 鹏 1931年9月生，江苏江阴人，现任中国书法家协会名誉主席，全国政协委员、中国文联荣誉委员、中国美术出版总社编审、艺委会顾问等，书法精行草，兼长隶、楷等多种书体。

润笔价格：35000~40000/平尺
供收藏家参考

Shen Peng, born in Jiangyin, Jiangsu Province, in September 1931, is Honorary President of China Calligraphers Association, member of the CPPCC, honorary member of China Federation of Literary and Art Circles, senior editor and consultant of Arts Committee of China Art Publishing House. He is skilled in running, clerical, and regular script.

Reference price: RMB35,000-40,000 per square feet

《少陵诗一首》 *A Poem by Du Fu*

中国当代书画名家作品收藏指南

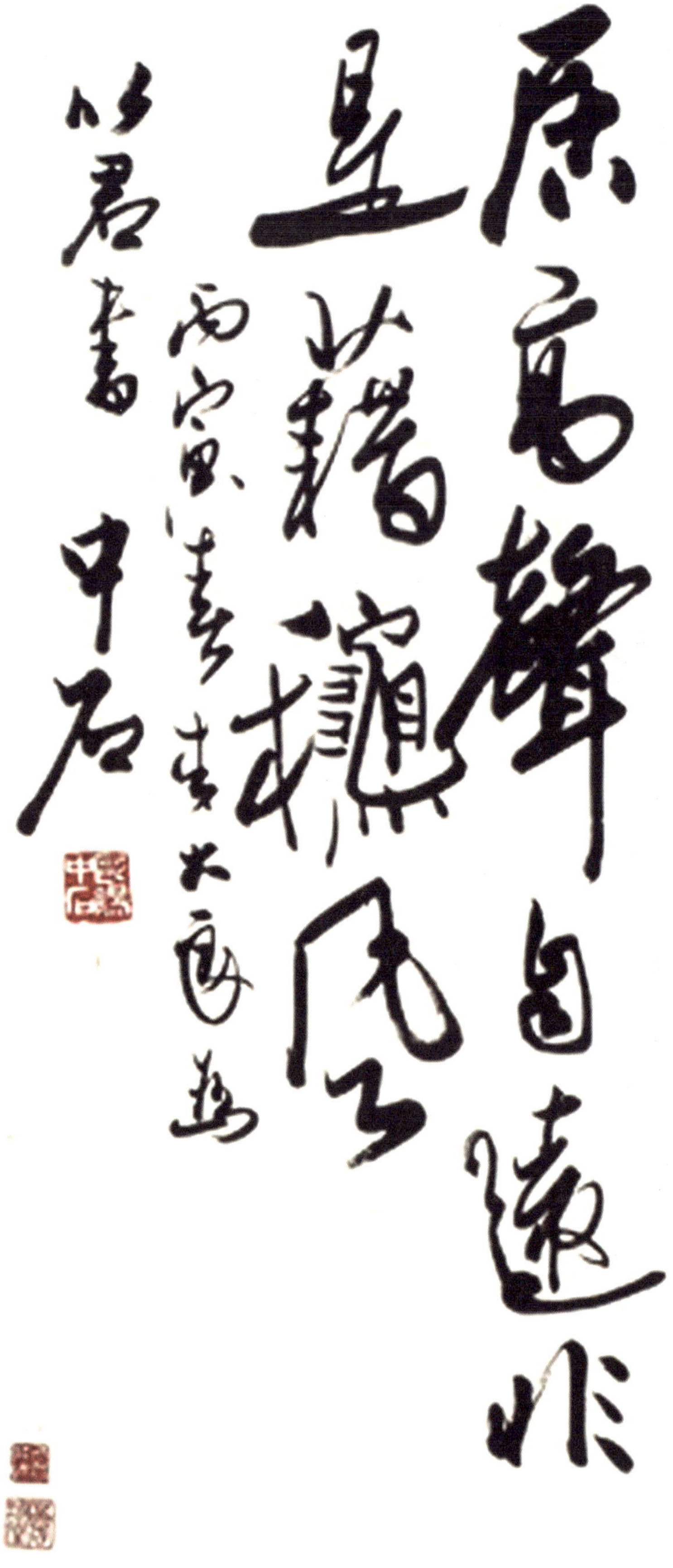

欧阳中石 OUYANG ZHONGSHI

欧阳中石 著名学者、书法家、书法教育家，生于1928年，山东省肥城人，现任首都师范大学教授、博士生博士后导师中国书法文化研究所所长、全国政协委员，中国书法家协会顾问，中国画研究院院务委员。

润笔价格：35000~40000/平尺
供收藏家参考

《行草条幅》 A Scroll of Semi-cursive Script

Ouyang Zhongshi, born in Feicheng, Shandong Province in 1928, is a famous scholar and calligrapher. He is now a professor (PhD supervisor) and Director of Chinese Calligraphy Art Institute with Capital Normal University, member of CPPCC, consultant of China Calligraphers Association, and council member of Chinese Painting Research Institute.

Reference price: RMB35,000-40,000 per square feet

李 铎
LI DUO

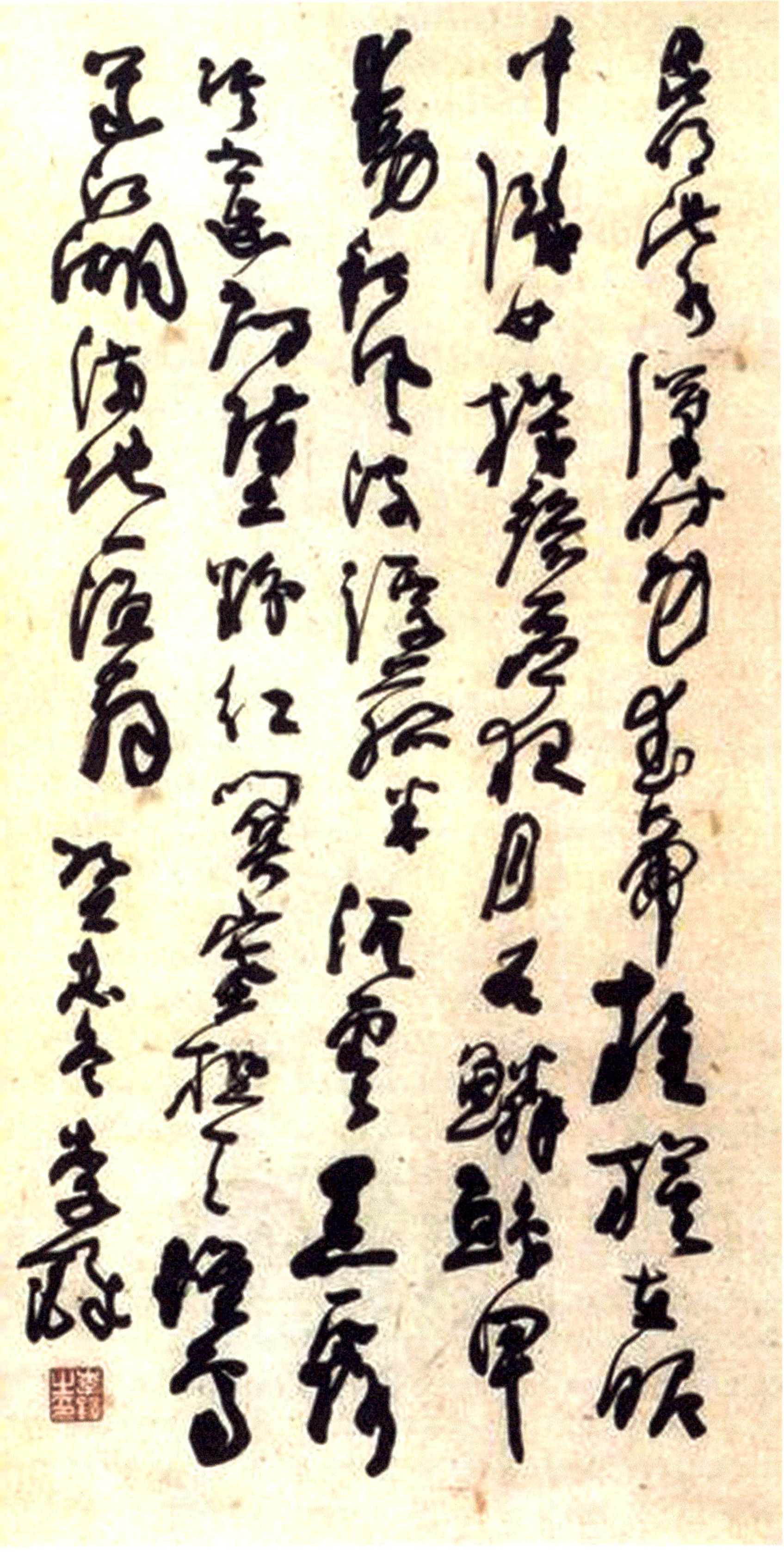

李 铎 将军，1930年4月生，湖南省醴陵市人，研究馆员，毕业于信阳步兵学院，文职将军，享受国家特殊津贴，全国著名书法家，现任全国政协委员、全国文联委员。

润笔价格：30000~35000/平尺
供收藏家参考

General Li Duo, born in Liling, Hunan Province, in April 1930, is a research librarian. A graduate of Xinyang Infantry Academy (now Jinan Military Academy), General Li receives Special Allowance of State Council of China. He is a nationally famous calligrapher, member of CPPCC and of China Federation of Literary and Art Circles.

Reference price: RMB30,000-35,000 per square feett

《草书条幅》
A Scroll of Running Script

权希军
QUAN XIJUN

权希军 1926年8月生，山东烟台市人，著名书法家，曾任中国书法家协会副秘书长，篆刻委员会副主任，刻字研究会会长，中国书法家协会顾问，中国文联书画艺术中心顾问。

润笔价格：20000~25000/平尺
供收藏家参考

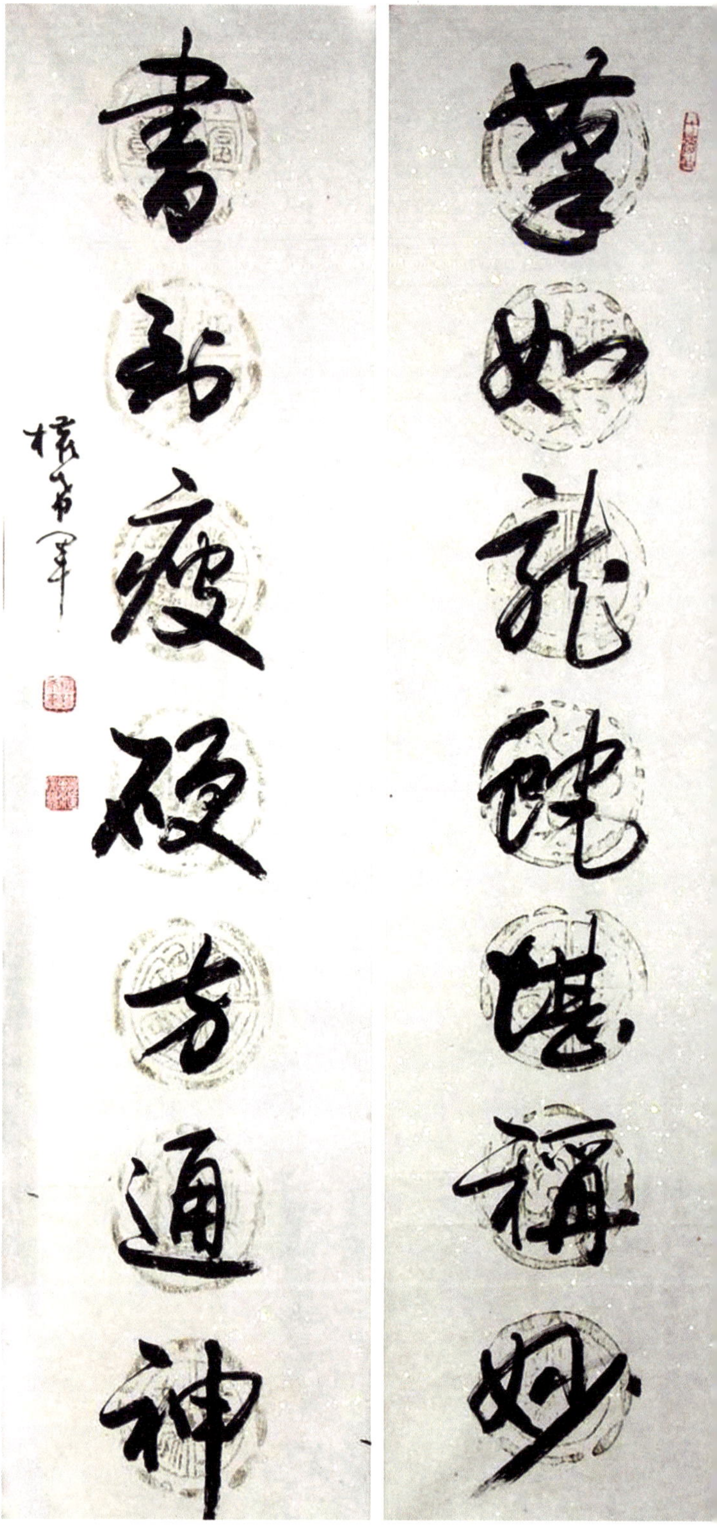

《对联》 A Couplet

Quan Xijun, born in Yantai, Shandong Province, in August 1926, is a famous calligrapher. He is the former Vice Secretary General of China Calligraphers Association, Vice Director of Seal Cutting Committee, President of Character Carving Research Society, and consultant of CCA, and consultant of Art Center of China Federation of Literary and Art Circles.

Reference price: RMB20,000-25,000 per square feet

田伯平 男，1958年出生，现任北京书法家协会驻会副主席兼秘书长，中国书法家协会理事兼教育委员会委员，中国人民大学国学院书法教授，北京市委党校成教院艺术总监。

润笔价格：12000~15000/平尺
供收藏家参考

田伯平
TAN BOPING

Tian Boping, born in 1958, is Vice President and Secretary General of Beijing Calligraphers Association, council member and member of Education Committee of China Calligraphers Association, Calligraphy Professor with School of Chinese Classics of China Renmin University, and Art Director of Adult School of Party School of Beijing Committee of CPC.

Reference price: RMB12,000-15,000 per square feet

《行草条幅》 *A Scroll of Semi-cursive Script*

张 飙 ZHANG BIAO

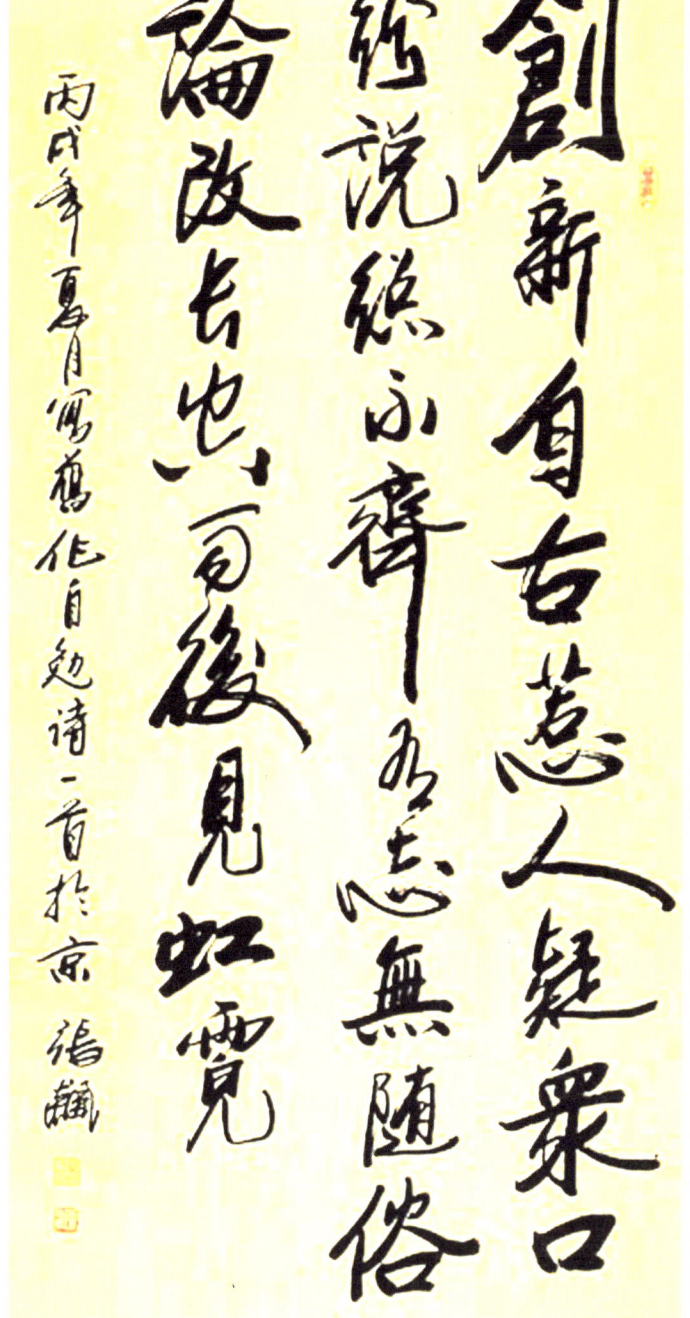

《自勉诗一首》 *A Self-encouraging Poem*

张　飙　男，1946 年 8 月生，中国书法家协会顾问，中国书法家协会中直分会会长，曾任中国书法家协会第四届驻会主席，分党组书记、评审委员会主任，中国文联第六届、第七届会委委员，曾任中国青年报副总编辑、科技日报总编辑，中国艺术报社长。

润笔价格：20000~25000/ 平尺
供收藏家参考

Zhang Biao, born in August 1946, is a consultant of China Calligraphers Association and President of Zhongzhi Branch of CCA. He is the 4th President, Party Secretary, and Director of Art Committee of CCA, member of the 6th and 7th committee of China Federation of Literary and Art Circles, former vice editor in chief of China Youth Daily, editor in chief of Science and Technology Daily, and President of China Art News.

Reference price: RMB15,000-20,000 per square feet

《毛泽东沁园春雪》 Snow by Mao Zedong

张铜彦　一九五八年十月出生，河北省高阳县人，现为中国书法家协会理事，中国金融书法家协会主席。

润笔价格：10000~12000/平尺
供收藏家参考

张铜彦
ZHANG TONGYAN

Zhang Tongyan, born in Gaoyang, Hebei Province, in October 1958, is a council member of China Calligraphers Association and President of China Financial Calligrapher Association

Reference price: RMB10,000-12,000 per square feet

马泰昌 1948年1月生,大学学历,清华大学美术学院当代艺术创作研究生,先后担任中国楹联学会副秘书长,中国国画家协会常务理事,中国书法家协会 分会 理事、会员,中石油书协理事。

润笔价格:5000~6000/平尺
供收藏家参考

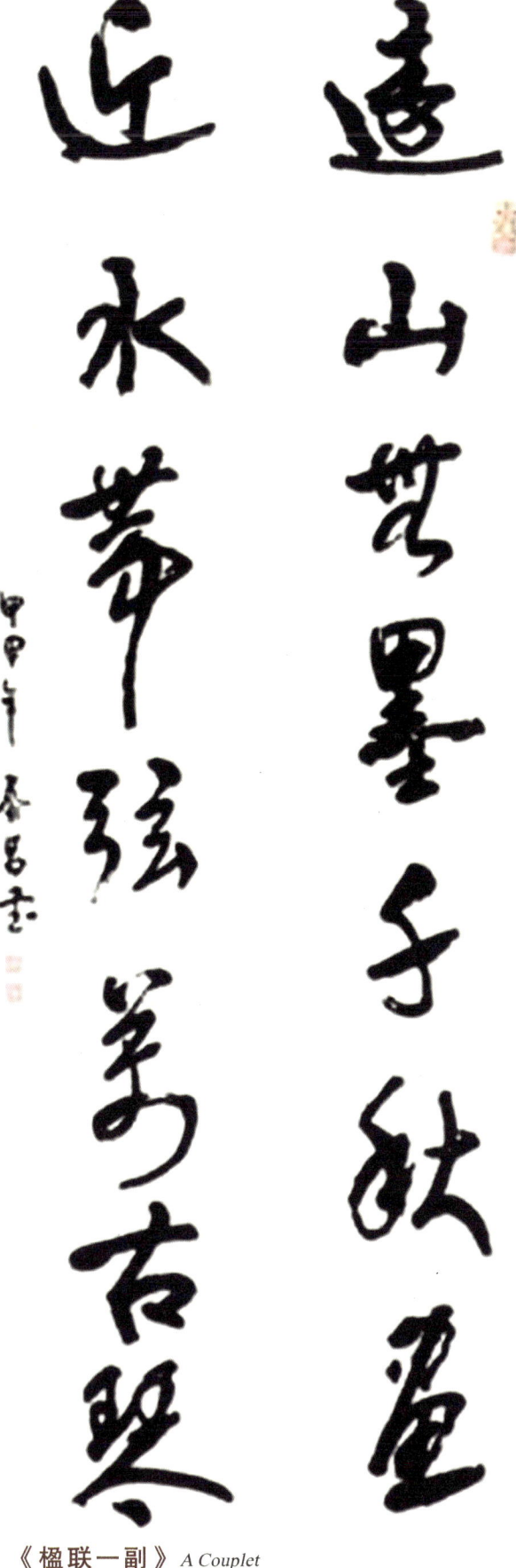

Ma Taichang, born in January 1948, is a postgraduate major in Contemporary Art from Academy of Arts and Design, Tsinghua University. He has held many positions, such as Vice Secretary General of Yinglian Society of China, standing council member of China Chinese Painting Association, council member and member of China Calligraphers Association's branch, and council member of China Petroleum Calligraphers Association.

Reference price: RMB5,000-6,000 per square feet

《楹联一副》 A Couplet

《郑板桥题画诗》
A Poem by Zheng Banqiao

邹德忠
ZOU DEZHONG

邹德忠 男 1938 年 2 月出生，山东烟台人，曾任中国书协组联部主任，中国书协第三届理事，现任中国书协中央国家机关分会副会长兼秘书长，中国书协书法培训中心教授。

润笔价格：15000~20000/ 平尺
供收藏家参考

Zou Dezhong, born in Yantai, Shandong Province, in February 1938, is former Director of Department of Organization and Liaison and used to be a council member of the 3rd committee of China Calligraphers Association. He is now Vice President and Secretary General of Central State Organ Branch of China Calligraphers Association and professor with Training Center of China Calligraphers Association.

Reference price: RMB15,000-20,000 per square feet

中国当代书画名家作品收藏指南

李元茂　1944年生于山西太原，现任海南省博物馆名誉馆长，国家一级美术师，国务院特贴专家，中国书法家协会鉴定评估委员会委员，海南省书协副主席。

润笔价格：10000~12000/平尺
供收藏家参考

李元茂 LI YUANMAO

Li Yuanmao, born in Taiyuan, Shanxi Province, in 1944, is Honorary President of Hainan Museum, National Class A artist, receiver of Special Allowance of State Council of China, member of Appraisal Committee of China Calligraphers Association, and Vice President of Hainan Calligraphers Association.

Reference price: RMB10,000-12,000 per square feet

《条幅》 A Scroll

李洪海
LI HONGHAI

《李白诗一首》 A Poem of Li Bai

李洪海

男，1946年1月生

天津市武清人

系中国书法家协会会员

中央直属机关书法协会会员

中韩书法联谊会常务理事

三峡画院特约教授

海南天涯咀名人馆艺术顾问

中国军事博物馆书画研究院副院长

中国国际友好联络会理事

润笔价格：10000~12000/平尺

供收藏家参考

Li Honghai, born in Wuqing, Tianjin, in January 1946, is a member of China Calligraphers Association and of Calligraphy Association of Central Organs of the CPC, standing council member of Sino-Korean Federation of Calligraphers, professor with Three Gorges Art Gallery, art consultant of Hainan Tianyacu Hall of Fame, Vice President of Calligraphy and Painting Gallery of Chinese Military History Museum, and council member of China Association for International Friendship Contact.

Reference price: RMB10,000-12,000 per square feet

中国当代书画名家作品收藏指南

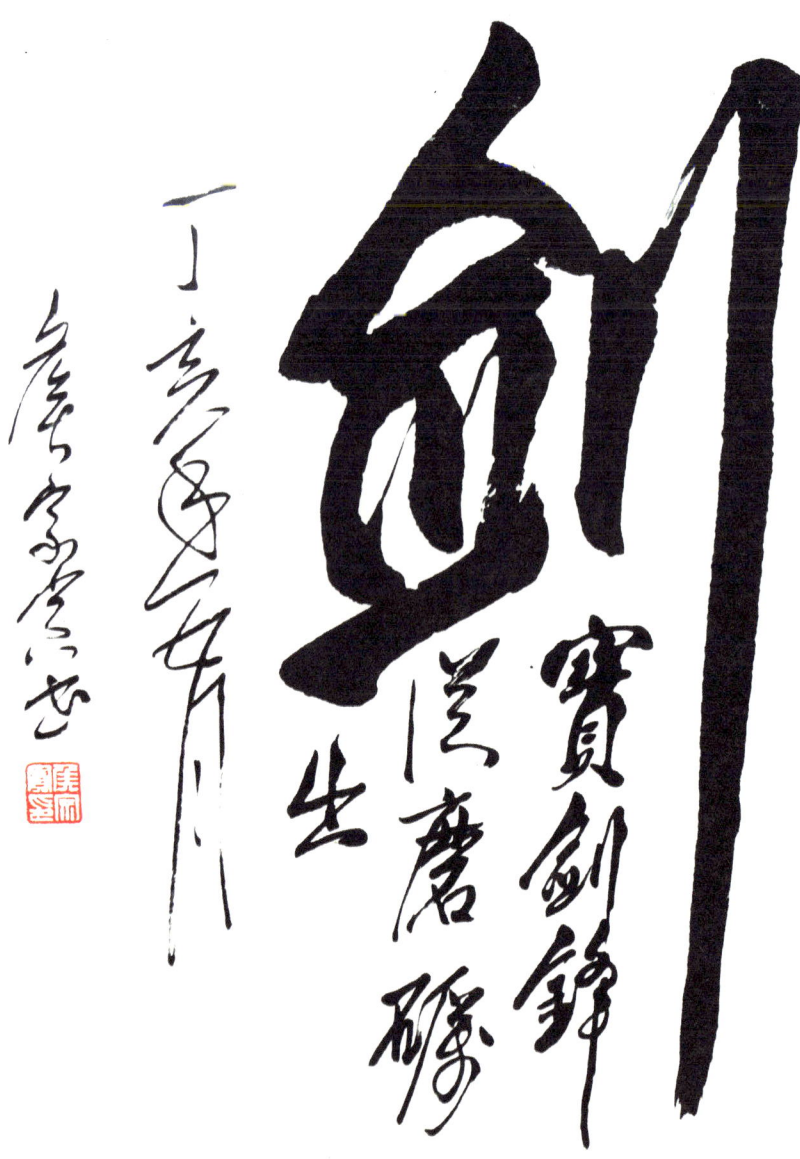

孟云飞 MENG YUNFEI

《宝剑锋从磨砺出》 Honing Makes a Sword Sharp

孟云飞 1972年8月出生于河南，1995年毕业于河南大学中文系并留校任教，2001年8月考入首都师范大学，中国书法文化研究所，师从著名学者、书法教育家欧阳中石先生，现供职于国务院参事室，中央文史研究馆，任《中华书画家》学术部主任，系中国文联特约研究员，中国书法家协会会员。

润笔价格：8000~10000/平尺
供收藏家参考

Meng Yunfei, born in Henan Province in August 1972, graduated from Department of Chinese Language and Culture of Henan University in 1955 and since then taught there until 2001. In August 2001, he was admitted to Chinese Calligraphy Art Institute of Capital Normal University where he became a student of famous scholar and calligrapher Ouyang Zhongshi. He now works in Counselors' Office of State Council and Central Research Institute of Culture and History. He is also Director of Academic Department of Chinese Calligraphers and Painters, researcher with China Federation of Literary and Art Circles, and member of China Calligraphers Association.

Reference price: RMB8,000-10,000 per square feet

苏士澎
SU SHIPENG

苏士澎 生于1949年3月，中国文物保护基金会副理事长，中国书协理事，中国书法家协会中央国家机关分会副会长。

润笔价格：8000~12000/平尺
供收藏家参考

Su Shipeng, born in March 1949, is Vice President of China Culture Relics Protection Foundation, council member of China Calligraphers Association, and Vice President of Central State Organ Branch of China Calligraphers Association.

Reference price: RMB8,000-12,000 per square feet

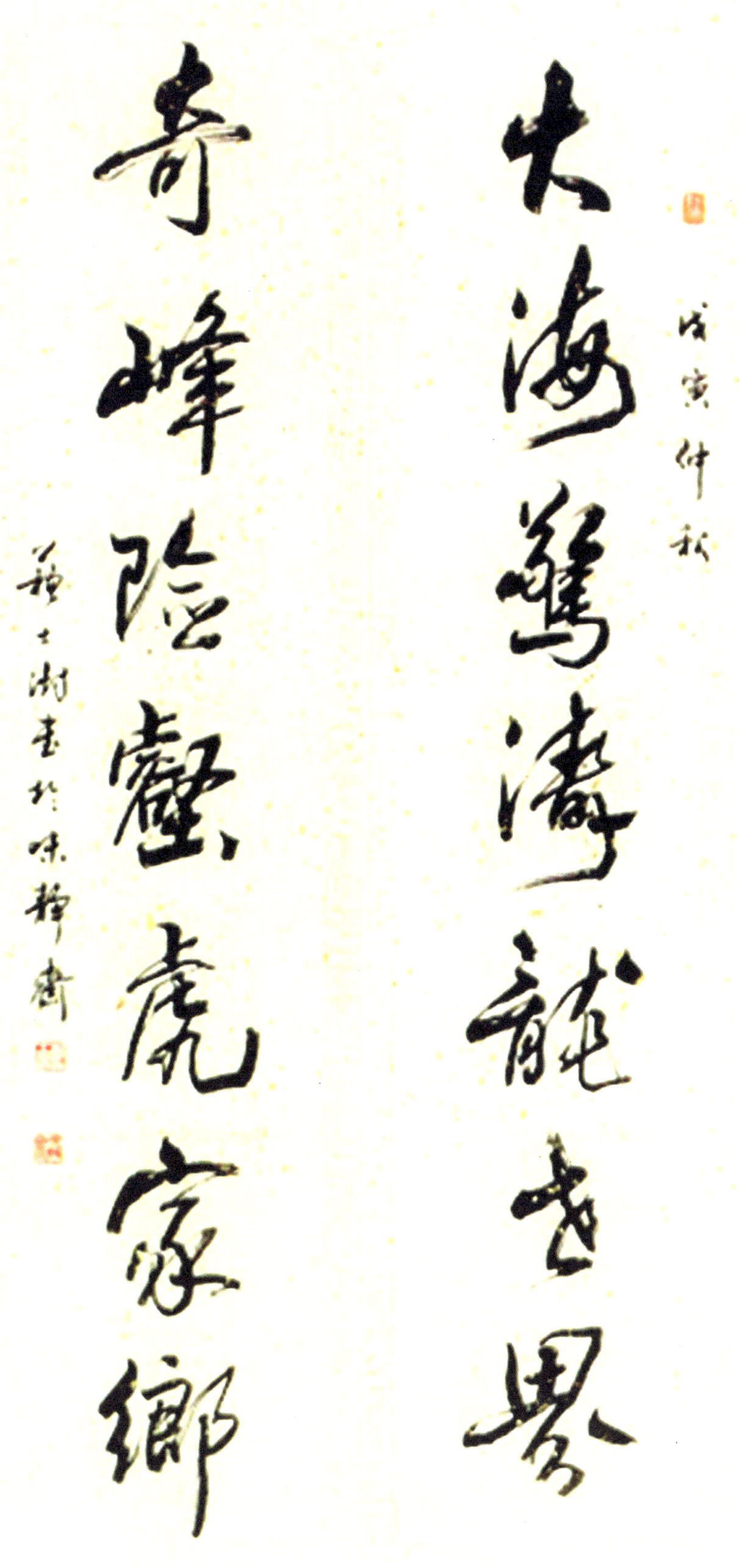

《对联》 A Couplet

刘庆石
LIU QINGSHI

刘庆石 男，黑龙江人，号黑水一鹤，艺名清石、明儒，斋号：文兴斋，现为中国书画院书法研究员。

润笔价格：2000~3000/ 平尺
供收藏家参考

Liu Qingshi, born in Heilongjiang Province and .with A Crane in Black Water, Qingshi, Mingru as his literary names, is a calligraphy researcher with China National Academy of Painting.

Reference price: RMB2,000-3,000 per square feet

《有感诗一首》 *A Poem of Sentiments*

《书法中堂》
A Large Vertical Scroll

| 张寿石
ZHANG SHOUSHI

张寿石 中国书法家协会会员，中国文联书画艺术交流中心理事，中国故宫博物院紫禁城书画协会理事。

润笔价格：8000~12000/平尺
供收藏家参考

Zhang Shoushi is a member of China Calligraphers Association, council member of Art Exchange Center of China Federation of Literary and Art Circles, and of Forbidden City Calligrapher and Painter Association of China's Palace Museum.

Reference price: RMB8,000-12,000 per square feet

袁胜聪 男，壮族，1954年12月生，广西美术家协会会员，中国书画家协会会员，中国书画研究院研究员。

润笔价格：3000~4000/平
尺供收藏家参考

袁胜聪
YUAN SHENGCONG

Yuan Shengcong, of Zhuang nationality, born in December 1954, is a member of Guangxi Artists Association, of China Calligrapher and Painter Association, and a researcher with China Calligraphy and Painting Research Institute.

Reference price: RMB3,000-4,000 per square feet

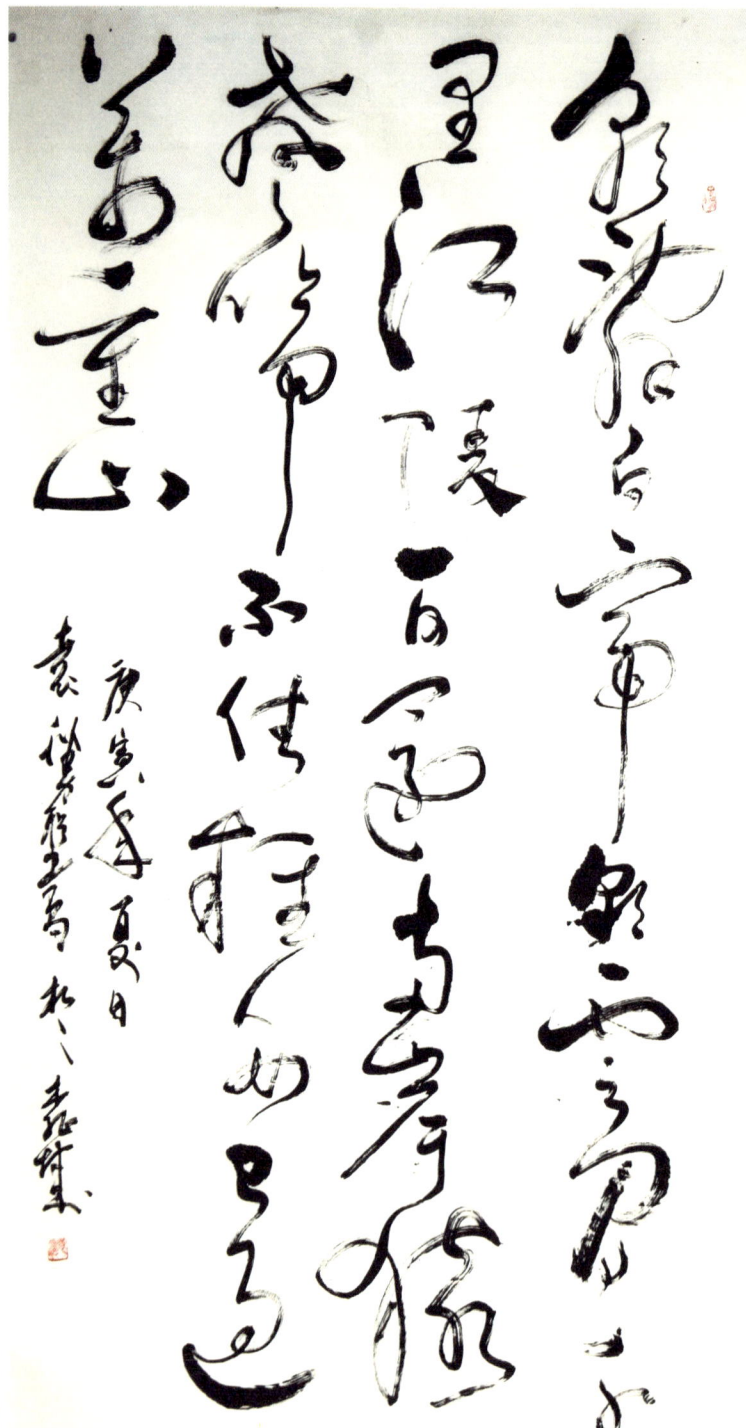

《草书条幅》
A Scroll of Cursive Script

《毛泽东诗词》 *A poem by Mao Zedong*

刘中方　男，1963年生，中国书画家联谊会会员，中国楹联学会会员，中国书画艺术研究院研究员。

润笔价格：3000~4000/平尺
供收藏家参考

Liu Zhongfang, born in 1963, is a member of China Calligrapher and Painter Federation, member of China Yinliang Society, and researcher with China Calligraphy and Painting Research Institute.

Reference price: RMB3,000-4,000 per square feet

尚 君
SHANG JUN

尚　君　名君，字随中，1965年出生于山东泰安，现为中国和韵文化产业传媒机构执行董事，中国书画艺术研究院副院长。

润笔价格：3000~4000/平尺
供收藏家参考

Shang Jun, born in Taian, Shandong Province and with Suizhong as his literary name, is Executive Director of China Heyun Culture Industry Media Framework Co., Ltd and Vice President of China Calligraphy and Painting Institute for Research.

Reference price: RMB3,000-4,000 per square feet

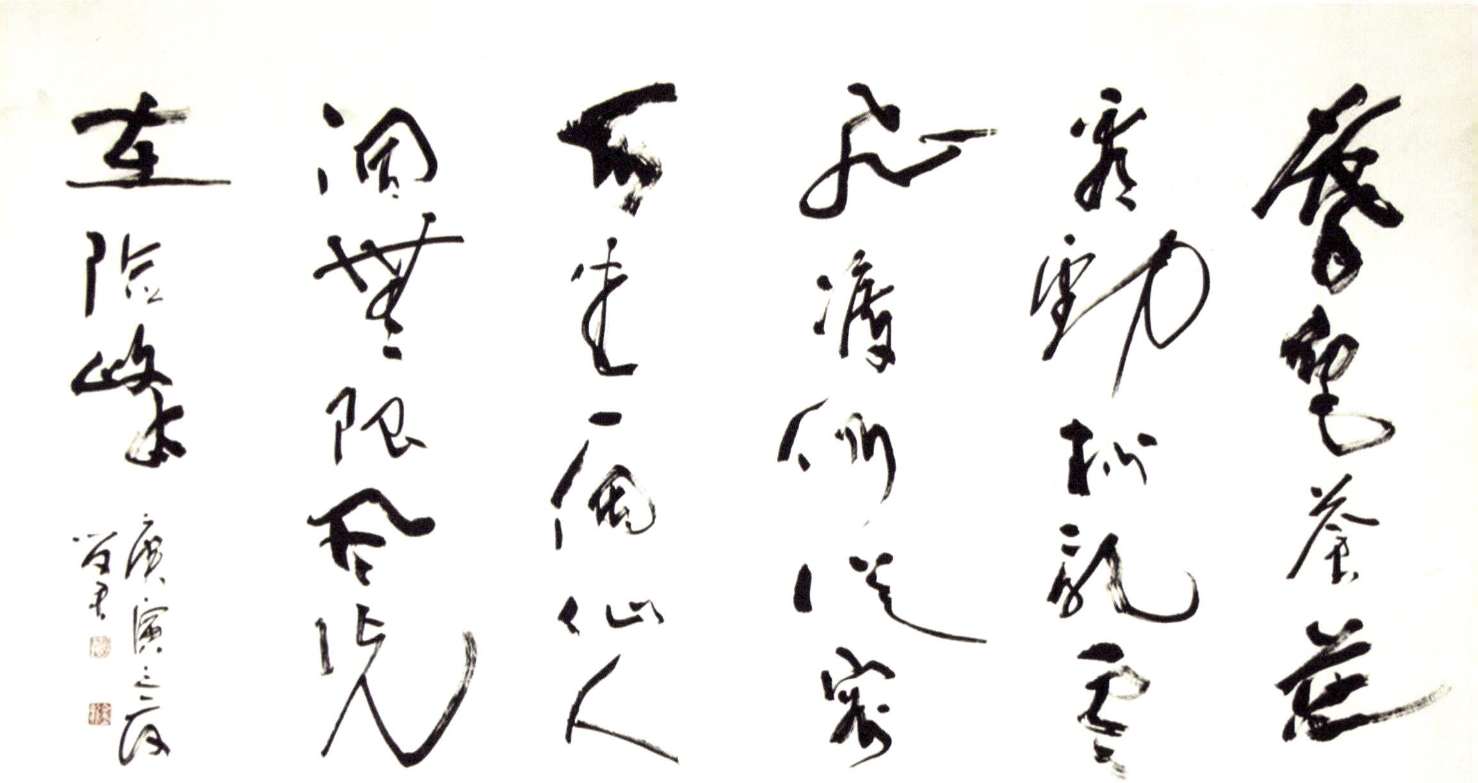

《毛泽东诗一首》 *A poem by Mao Zedong*

《博爱》 Universal Philanthropy

白银禄
BAI YINLU

白银禄 又名云露，1939年生于河北省石家庄市，历任中国长城书画院画家，中国榜书艺术研究会会员，中国美术家协会河北分会会员。

润笔价格：3000~4000/平尺
供收藏家参考

Bai Yinlu, also known as Yunlu, born in Shijiazhuang, Hebei Province, in 1939, is a painter with China Great Wall Calligraphy and Painting Gallery, member of China Bangshu Art Research Society, and of Hebei Branch of China Artists Association.

Reference price: RMB3,000-4,000 per square feet

白云霄
BAI YUNXIAO

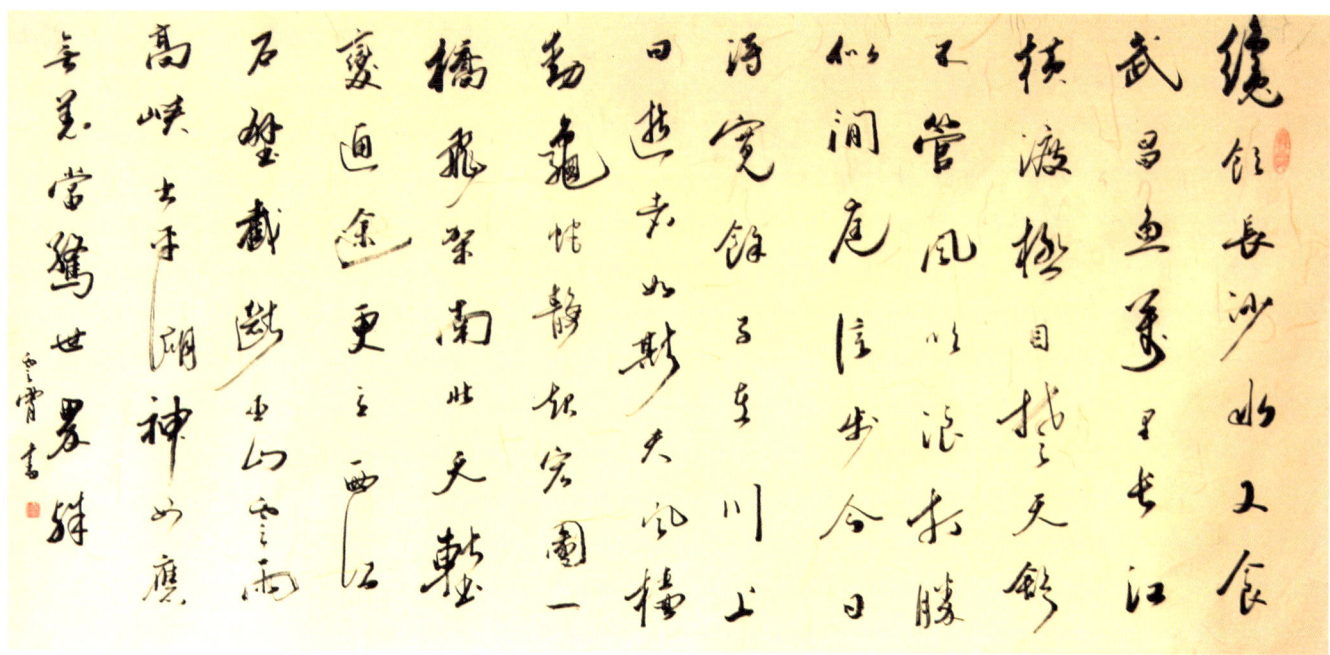

《毛泽东诗词》 97*180　　A poem by Mao Zedong 97*180

白云霄　男，蒙古族，1968年生于辽宁康平县，包头市书法家协会会员。

润笔价格：2000~3000/平尺
供收藏家参考

Bai Yunxiao, of Mongolian nationality, born in Kangping, Liaoning Province, in 1968, is a member of Baotou Calligraphers Association.

Reference price: RMB2,000-3,000 per square feet

蔡正雅
CAI ZHENGYA

蔡正雅　男，汉族，1948年12月生，江西省莲花人，现为江西省美术家协会会员，中国书法家协会权益保障委员会委员，江西书法家协会副主席，萍乡市书法家协会主席。

润笔价格：5000~6000/平尺
供收藏家参考

Cai Zhengya, born in Lianhua, Jiangxi Province, in December 1948, is a member of Jiangxi Artists Association, member of Interest and Right Protection Committee of China Calligraphers Association, Vice President of Jiangxi Calligraphers Association, and President of Pingxiang Calligraphers Association.

Reference price: RMB4,000-5,000 per square feet

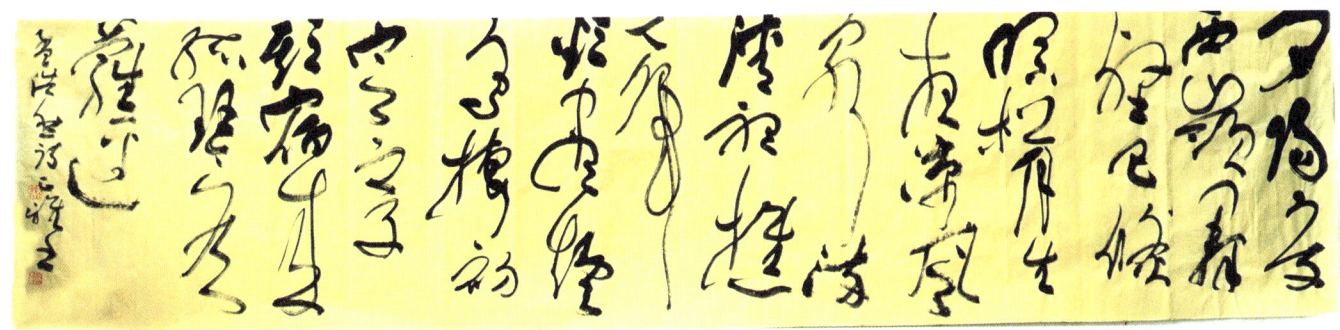

《孟浩然诗一首》 *A Poem by Meng Haoran*

陈科粟 CHEN KESU

陈科粟 男，1976年10月出生，广东省汕头市潮阳区人，号"半悟"，广东省汕头市书法家协会会员。

润笔价格：3000~4000/平尺
供收藏家参考

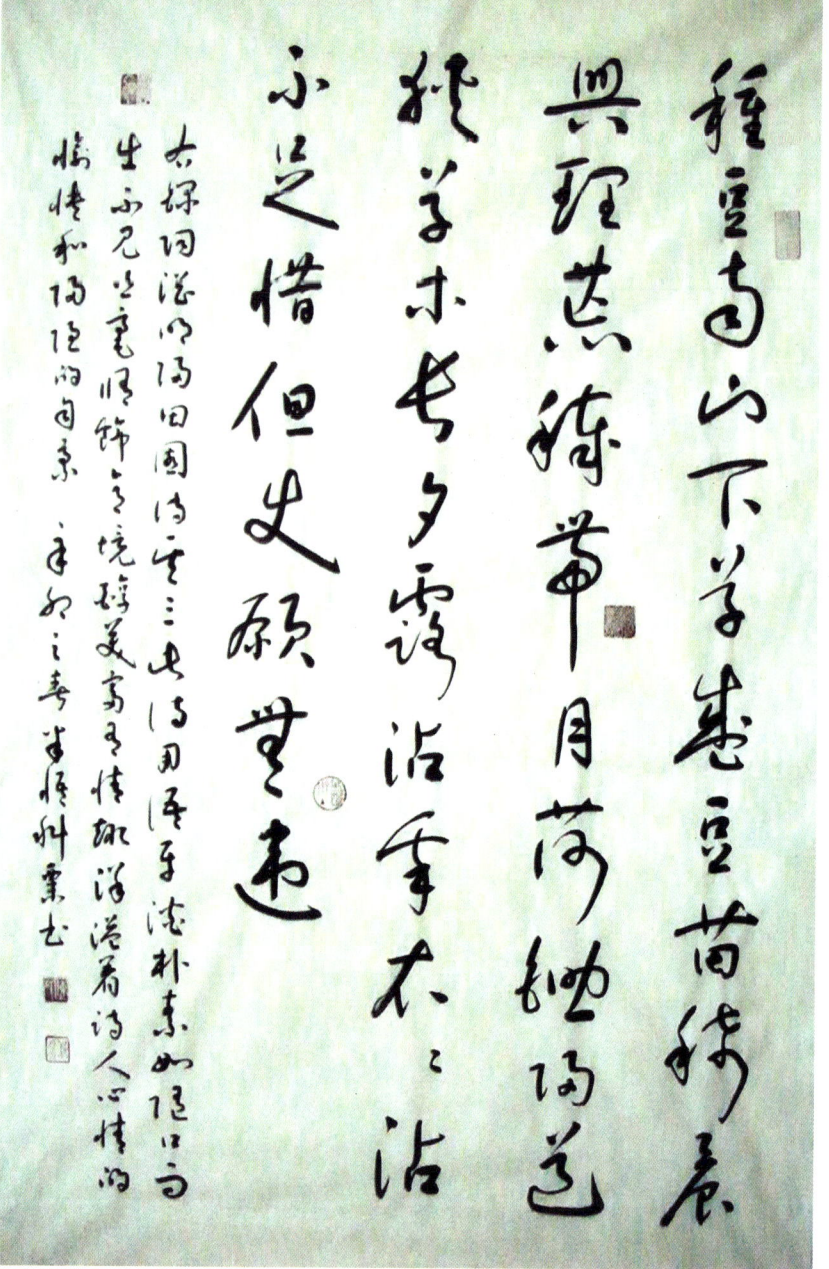

《行草条幅》 *A Scroll of Semi-cursive Script*

Chen Kesu, born in Shantou, Guangdong Province, in October 1976, and with Banwu (Almost Understanding) as his literary name, is a member of Shantou Calligraphers Association.

Reference price: RMB3,000-4,000 per square feet

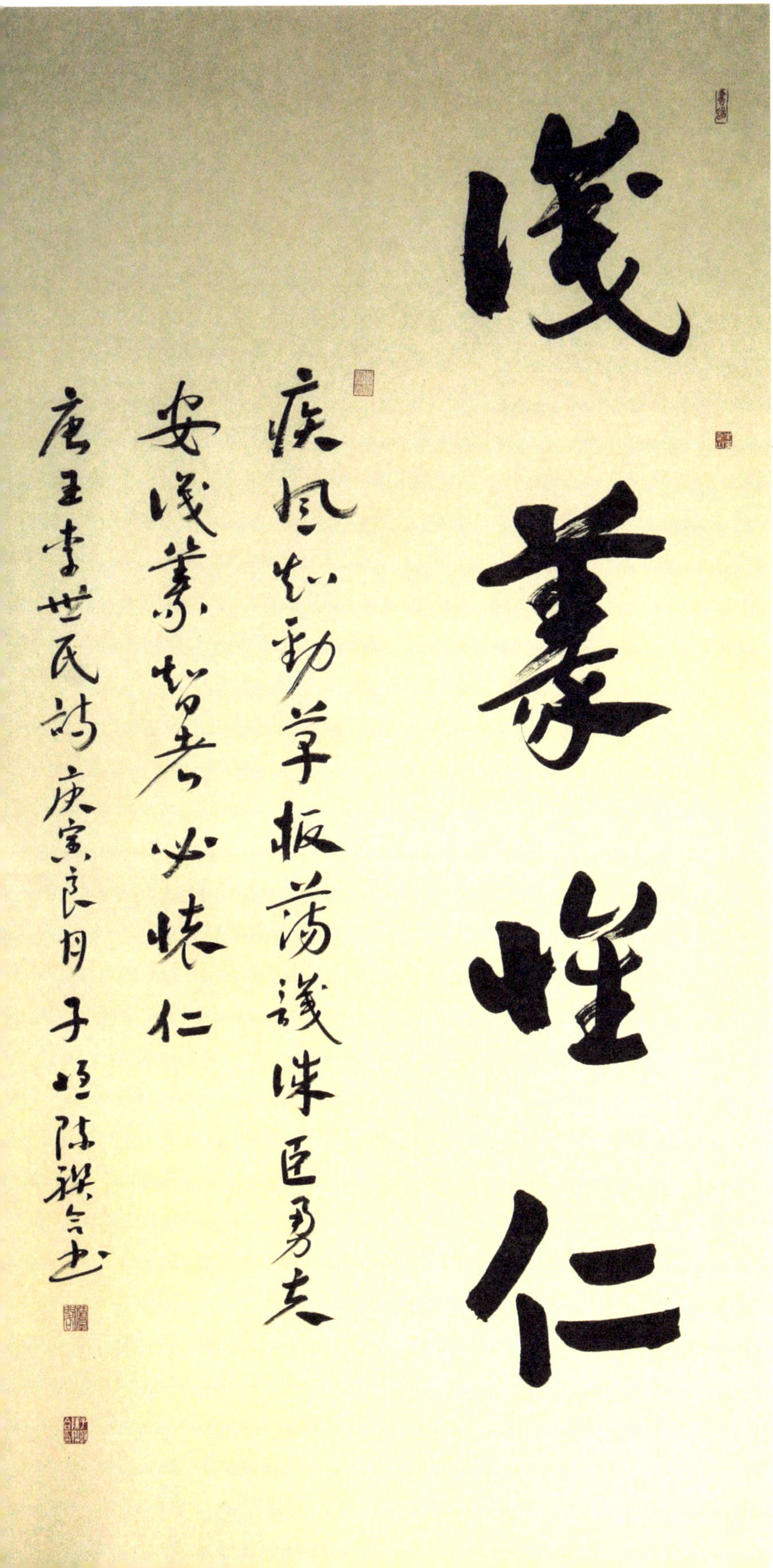

陈联合
CHEN LIANHE

《识篆惟仁》180*96
Shi Zhuan Wei Ren (Benevolent People Understand Seal Script) 180*96

陈联合 海军某部主任，中国书法家协会会员，中国楹联协会常务理事，教授，评委。

润笔价格：7000~8000/平尺
供收藏家参考

Chen Lianhe, a naval officer and professor, is a member of China Calligraphers Association, and council member of China Yinglian Society.

Reference price: RMB7,000-8,000 per square feet

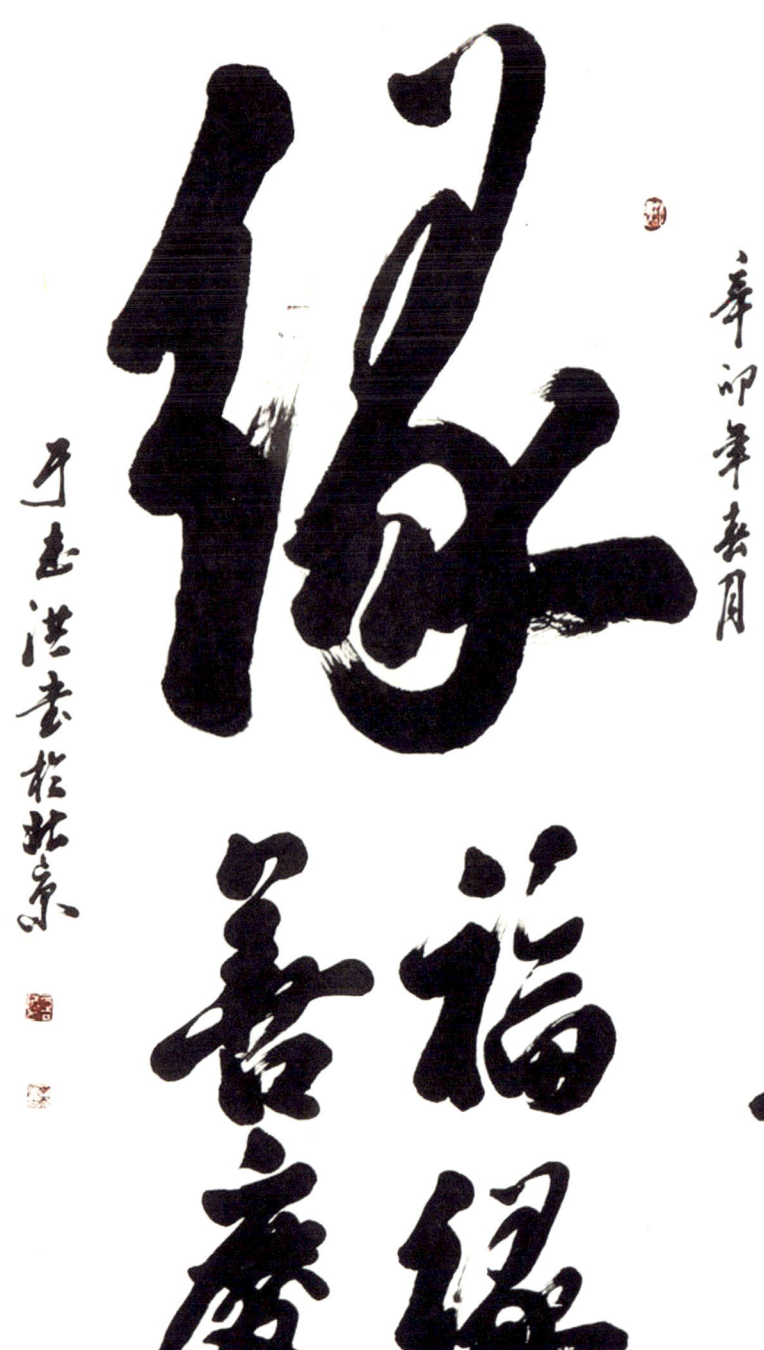

于志洪
YU ZHIHONG

《楹联一副》 A Couplet

于志洪　男，1948年生，北京市书法家协会会员，中国书画研究院理事，燕京书法研究会会员。

润笔价格：3000~5000/平尺
供收藏家参考

Yu Zhihong, born in 1948, is a member of Beijing Calligraphers Association, council member of China Calligraphy and Painting Research Institute, and member of Yanjing Calligraphy Research Society.

Reference price: RMB3,000-5,000 per square feet

杜思吾
DU SIWU

杜思吾　中国书法家协会会员，中国国画家协会理事，文化部中国书画创作基地专职书画家，清华美院毛国典书法工作室助教。

润笔价格：5000~6000/平尺
供收藏家参考

Du Siwu is a member of China Calligraphers Association, council member of China Chinese Painting Association, professional calligrapher and painter with China Calligraphy and Painting Creation Base of Ministry of Culture, and teaching assistant in Mao Guodian Calligraphy Studio of Academy of Arts and Design, Tsinghua University.

Reference price: RMB5,000-6,000 per square feet

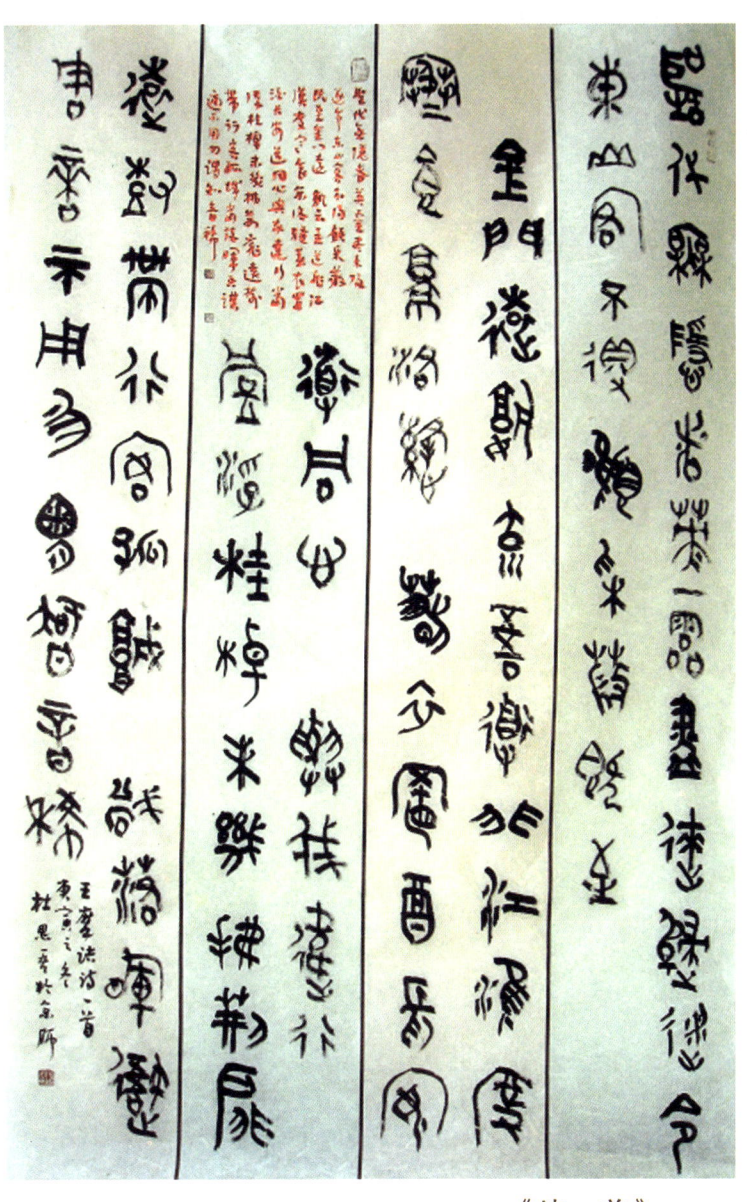

《诗一首》 A Poem

范海军
FAN HAIJU

范海军 1935年5月生,黑龙江省宁安市人,书法家,中国书画家协会会员,吉林名人文化研究院院士副主席,中华书画研究会名誉教授。

润笔价格:4000~5000/平尺
供收藏家参考

《净魂》Clear Soul

Fan Haiju, born in Anning, Heilongjiang Province, in May 1935, is a calligrapher. He is a member of China Calligrapher and Painting Association, Vice President of Jilin Celebrity Culture Research Institute, and Honorary Professor with China Calligraphy and Painting Research Institute.

Reference price: RMB4,000-5,000 per square feet

《篆书陶渊明诗一首》97*180 *A Poem by Tao Yuanming in Seal Script*

国世晓
GUO SHIXIAO

国世晓 1940年，青岛市书法家协会会员，山东省书法家协会会员，北京市中韩书法家联谊会会员。

润格：3000~5000/平尺
供收藏家参考

Guo Shixiao, born in 1940, is a member of Qingdao Calligraphers Association, of Shandong Calligraphers Association, and of Sino-Korean Federation of Calligraphers.

Reference price: RMB3,000-5,000 per square feet

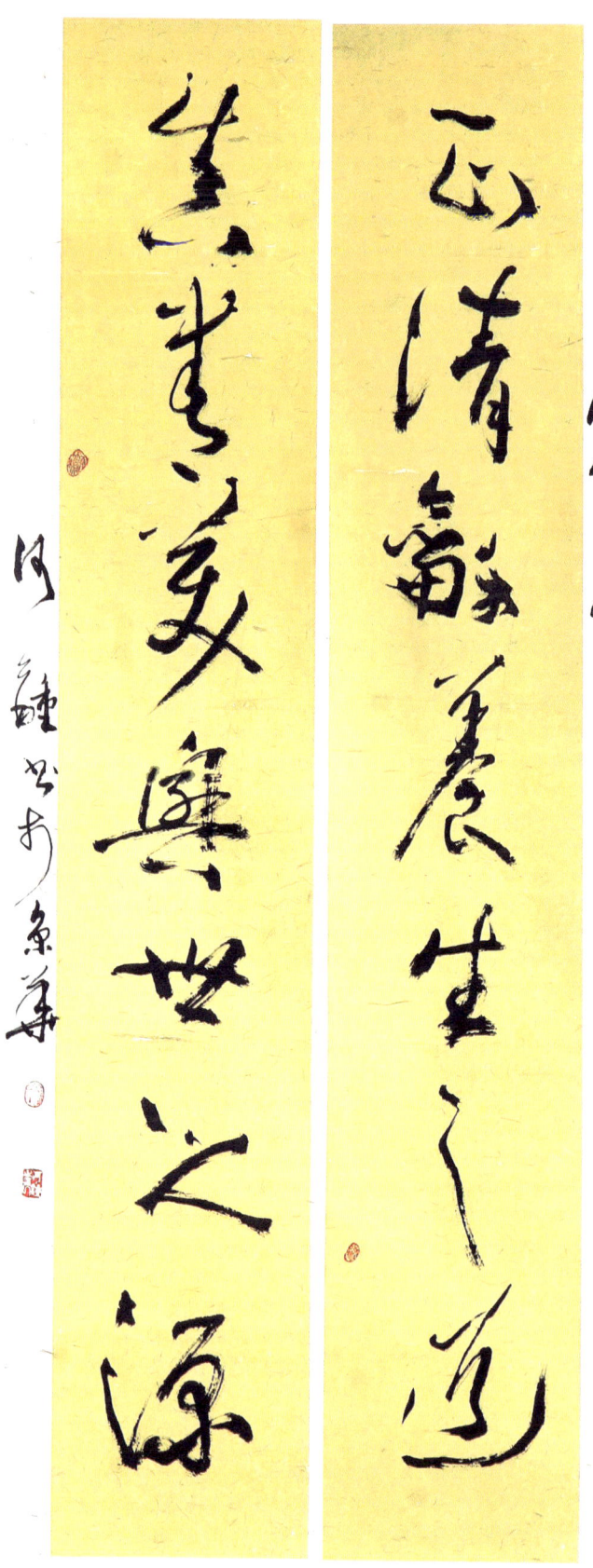

《行草对联》 *A Couplet in Semi-cursive Scrpit*

何　钟　出生于北京，中国书法家协会会员，中国楹联学会，中国榜书研究会，中国古琴研究会，北京京胡研究会会员。

润格：5000~6000/平尺
供收藏家参考

何钟
He Zhong

He Zhong, born in Beijing, is a member of China Calligraphers Association, of China Yinglian Society, of China Bangshu Rrt Research Society, of China Ancient Qin Research Society, and of Beijing Jinghu Research Society.

Reference price: RMB5,000-6,000 per square feet

胡 韵
HU YUN

胡 韵 1967年生于浙江湖州，中国艺术研究院研究生院中国画研究生创作课程班毕业，浙江省美术家协会会员，浙江省书法家协会会员，浙江省中国花鸟画家协会会员。

润笔价格：4000~5000/平尺
供收藏家参考

Hu Yun, born in Huzhou, Zhejiang Province in 1967, is a graduate from Program of Postgraduate Creation of Graduate School of Chinese National Academy of Arts, member of Zhejiang Artists Association, of Zhejiang Calligraphers Association, and of Zhejiang Bird-and-Flower Painters Association.

Reference price: RMB4,000-5,000 per square feet

《金文集字》
A Collection of Bronze Ware Script

樊宏涛 FAN HONGTAO

樊宏涛 男，1964年9月生于，河南省孟津县老城乡（现会盟镇）雷河村，现任孟津县王铎书法馆馆长，洛阳市书协理事，河南省书法家协会会员，孟津县书协主席。

润笔价格：4000~5000/平尺
供收藏家参考

Fan Hongtao, born in Leihe Village, Laocheng Town (now Huimeng Town), Mengjin County, Henan Province in September 1964, is Curator of Wang Duo Calligraphy Gallery in Mengjin, council member of Luoyang Calligraphers Association, member of Henan Calligraphers Association, and President of Mengjin Calligraphers Association.

Reference price: RMB4,000-5,000 per square feet

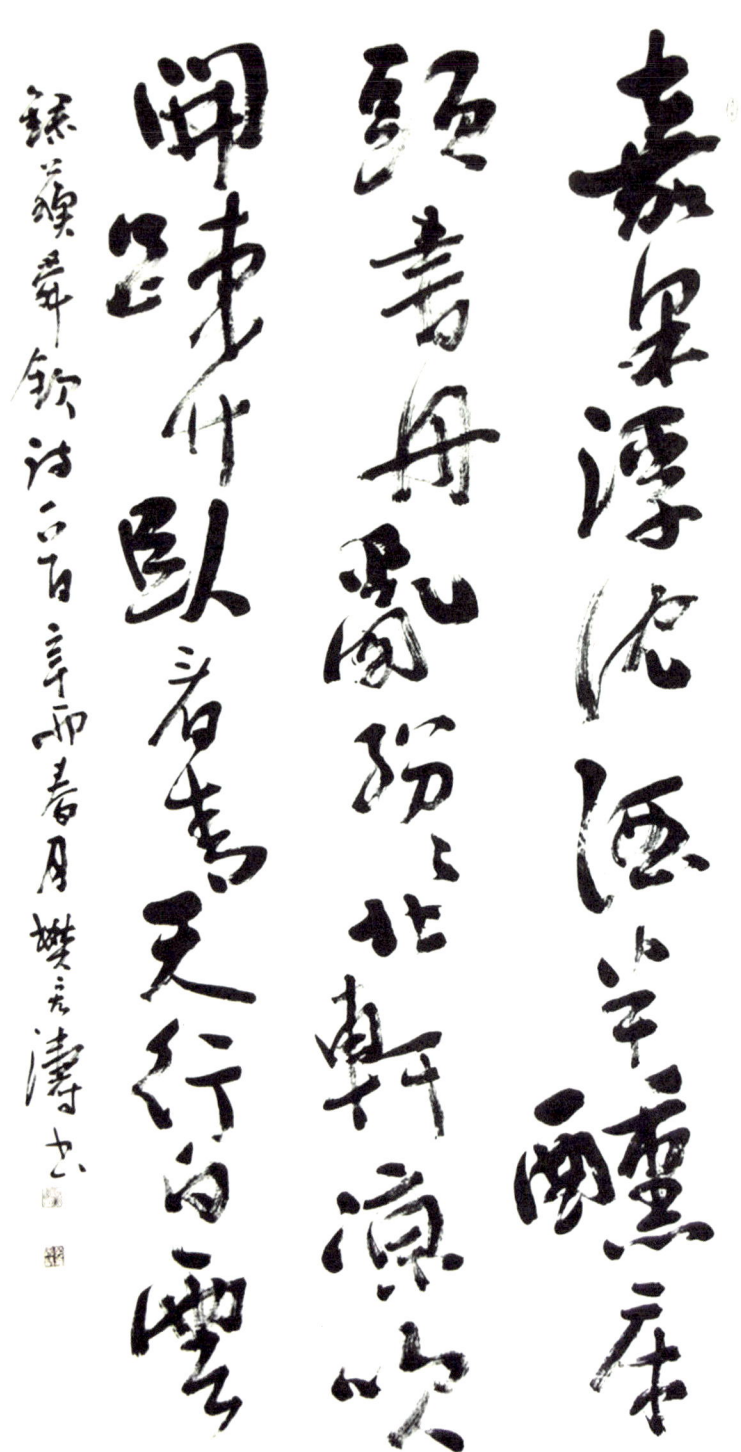

《苏舜钦诗一首》 A Poem by Su Shunqin

刘世铮
LIU SHIZHENG

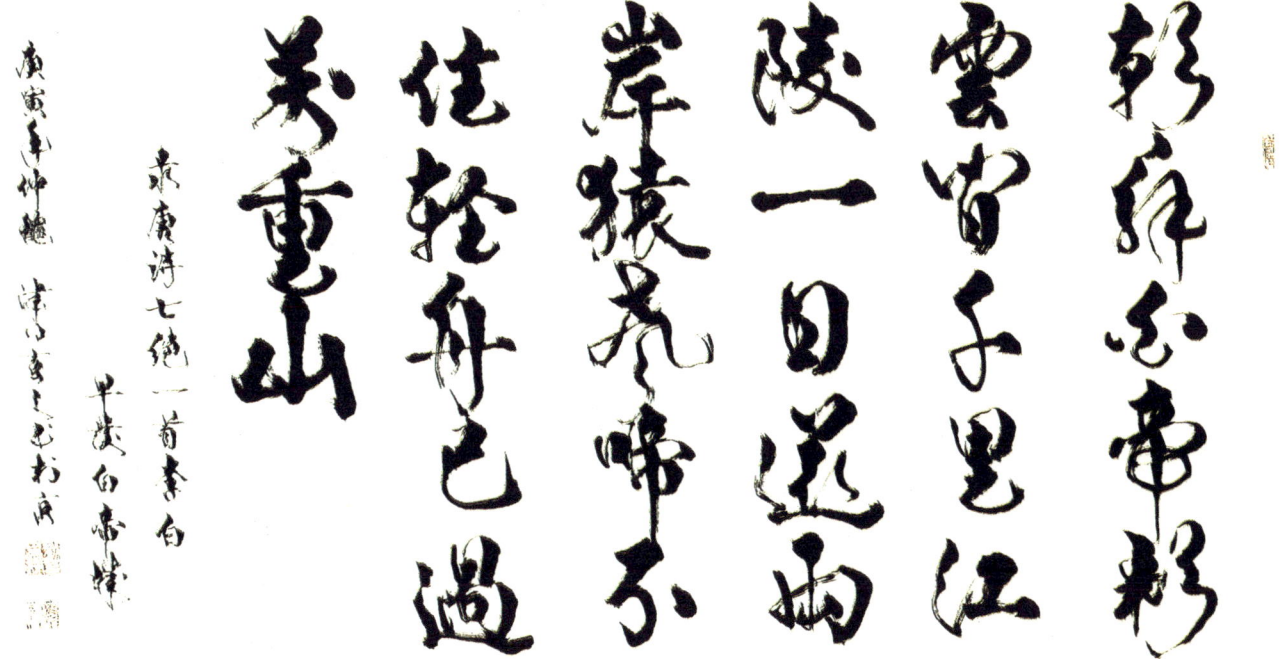

《李白诗一首》97*180　A Poem by Li Bai 97*180

刘世铮　1939年生，中国老年书画研究会研究员，中华艺术学会北京地区执行长，中国书画研究院高级研究员，毛泽东思想学术研究会书画院院士，文化部诗酒文化协会书画院特邀高级顾问。

润笔价格：2000~3000/平尺
供收藏家参考

Liu Shizheng, born in 1939, is a researcher with China Calligraphy and Painting Research Society for the Aged, Executive Director of China Art Society for Beijing, senior researcher with China Calligraphy and Painting Research Institute, member of Painting and Calligraphy Gallery of Mao Zedong Thoughts Research Society, and senior consultant of Painting and Calligraphy of Poetry and Wine Culture Association of Ministry of Culture.

Reference price: RMB2,000-3,000 per square feet

叶昌明　1951年出生，南京人，南京市美术家协会会员，南京市书法家协会会员，南京市花鸟研究会会员。

润笔价格：3000~4000/平尺
供收藏家参考

Ye Changming, born in Nanjing in 1951, is a member of Nanjing Artists Association, of Nanjing Calligraphers Association, and of Nanjing Bird-and-Flower Painting Research Society.

Reference price: RMB3,000-4,000 per square feet

《条幅》 A Scroll

庞舜尧
PANG SHUNYAO

庞舜尧 又名庞亚，1964年生于重庆市，中国书法家协会会员，北京中国画院花鸟部副主任。

润笔价格：4000~5000/平尺
供收藏家参考

Pang Shunyao, also known as Pang Ya, born in Chongqing in 1964, is a member of China Calligraphers Association and Vice Director of Department of Bird-and-Flower Painting of CIAA.

Reference price: RMB3,000-4,000 per square feet

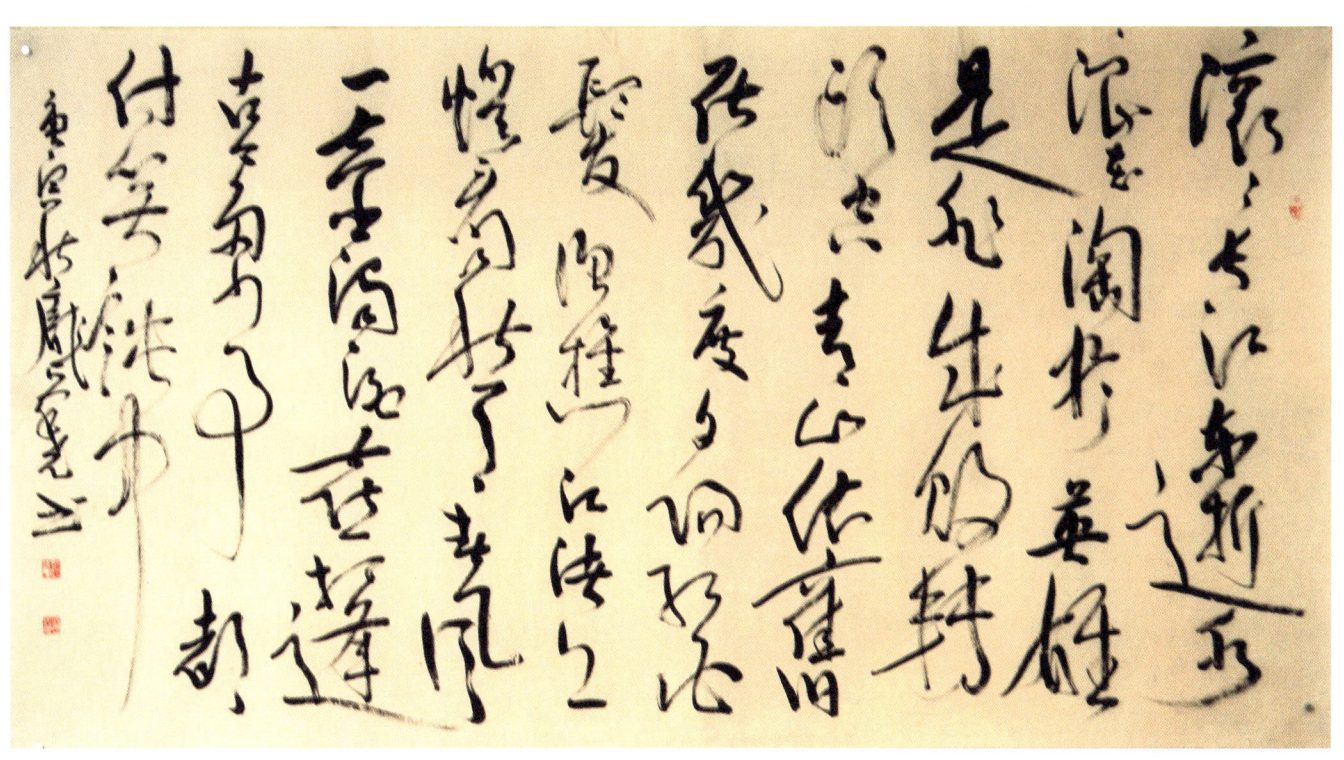

《三国演义开篇词》 Opening Poem of Romance of Three Kingdoms

中国当代书画名家作品收藏指南

彭义浔 1951年生,中国当代书画家,中国书法家协会会员,江西省书法家协会理事会员,九江市艺术家协会副秘书长。

润笔价格:4000~5000/平尺
供收藏家参考

彭义浔 PENG YIXUN

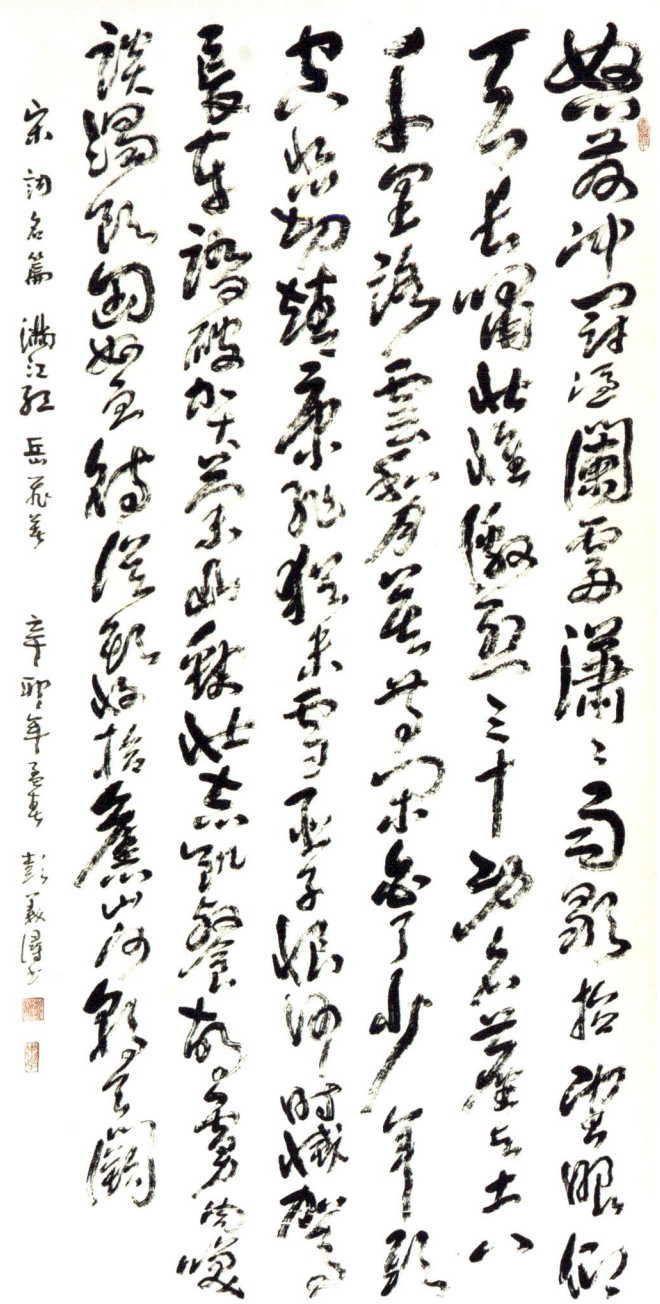

《满江红》 Man Jiang Hong by Yue Fei

Peng Yixun, a contemporary Chinese painter born in 1951, is a member of China Calligraphers Association, council member of Jiangxi Calligraphers Association, and Vice Secretary General of Jiujiang Artists Association.

Reference price: RMB4,000-5,000 per square feet

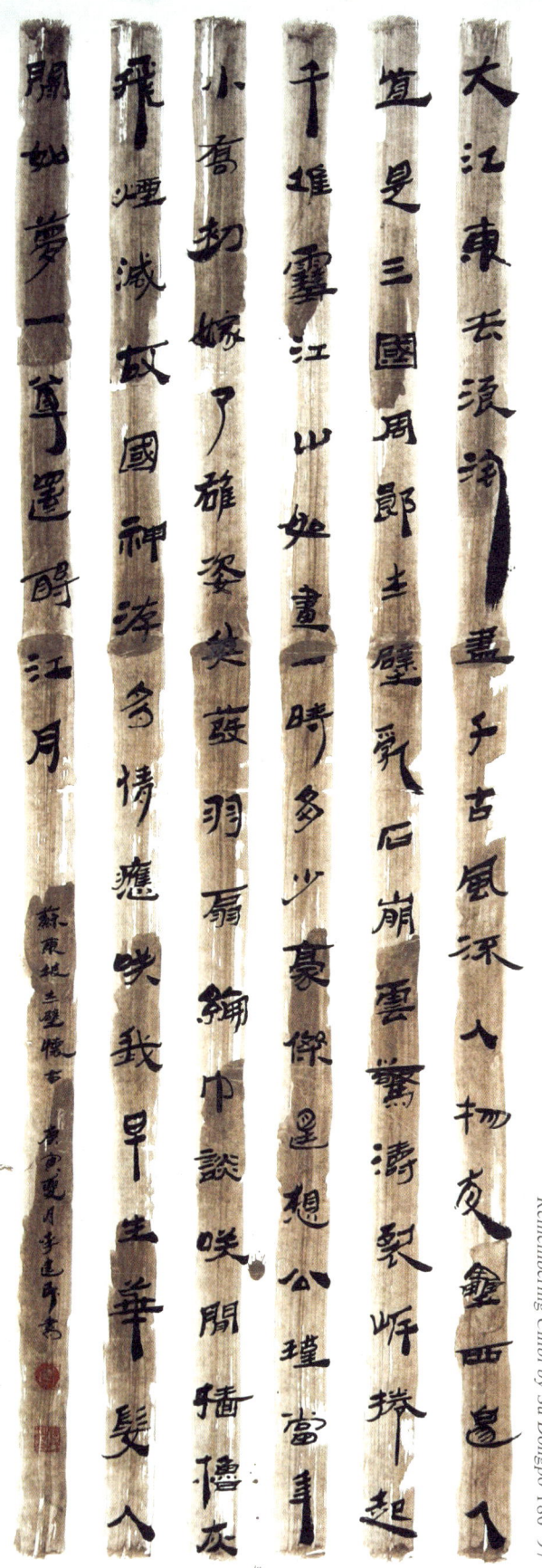

《苏东坡 赤壁怀古》180*97
Remembering Chibi by Su Dongpo 180*97

李建民
LI JIANMIN

李建民 1956生，男，中国国画院书法创作委员会副主席，甘肃诗书画联谊会常务理事，甘肃书画家协会副主席，甘肃省美协会员，甘肃省书法家协会会员。

润笔价格：8000~10000/平
供收藏家参考

Li Jianmin, born in 1956, is Vice President of Calligraphy Creation Committee of China Traditional Chinese Painting Institute, standing council member of Gansu Poetry, Calligraphy and Painting Federation, Vice President of Gansu Painters Association, member of Gansu Artists Association and of Gansu Calligraphers Association.

Reference price: RMB8000-10000 per square feet

柴建方
CHAI JIANFANG

柴建方 1943年12月出生，河南郸城人，宁夏书协名誉主席，国家一级美术师。

润笔价格：5000~6000/平尺
供收藏家参考

Chai Jianfang, born in Dancheng, Henan Province, in December 1943, is Honorary President of Xingnia Calligraphers Association, and a National Class A artist.

Reference price: RMB3000-4000 per square feet

《鲁迅先生诗一首》178*72.5
*A Poem by Mr. Lu Xun 178*72.5*

杜富华 男，1947年生，中国书画家协会副主席，中国书协培训中心。

润笔价格：2000~2500/平尺
供收藏家参考

杜富华
DU FUHUA

Du Fuhua, born in 1947, is Vice President of China Calligrapher and Painter Association and member of Training Center of China Calligraphers Association.

Reference price: RMB2000-2500 per square feet

《千字文》180*97　1000 Character Classic 180*97

中国当代书画名家作品收藏指南

《中华世纪坛铭文》 97*180　　*Epigraph of China Millennium Monument 97*180*

巩子之 GONG ZIZHI

巩子之 男，1946年生，淄博市书画研究会会员，山东省老年书画研究会会员，中国书画研究院艺术委员会委员。

润笔价格：2000~3000/平尺
供收藏家参考

Gong Zizhi, born in 1946, is a member of Zibo Calligraphy and Painting Research Society, of Shandong Calligraphy and Painting Research Society for the Aged, and of Arts Committee of China Calligraphy and Painting Research Institute.

Reference price: RMB2000-3000 per square feet

《爱莲说》97*180　*Ode to Lotus Flower 97*180*

马 程
MA CHENG

马　程　回族，1956年3月出生，书法专业教师
北京市书法家协会会员。

润笔价格：3000~4000/平尺
供收藏家参考

Ma Cheng, of Hui nationality and born in March 1956, is a calligraphy teacher and member of Beijing Calligraphers Association.

Reference price: RMB2000–3000 per square feet

邱 忠
QIU ZHONG

邱　忠　湖南省书协会员，中国书法艺术研究院艺委会会员，中国教育学会书法教育专业委员会会员，北京卿云书画院、广西炎黄书画院院士。

润笔价格：3000~4000/平尺
供收藏家参考

Qiu Zhong is a member of Hunan Calligraphers Association, member of Arts Committee of China Calligraphy Research Institute, member of Calligraphy Education Committee of Chinese Society of Education, member of Beijing Qingyun Calligraphy and Painting Gallery, and member of Guangxi Yanhuang Painting Gallery.

Reference Price: RMB 3,000-4,000 per square feet

《隶书条幅》180*96
A Scroll of Clerical Script

苏林艺高
SU LINYIGAO

《滚滚长江东逝水》 *Yangtze River Flowing East*

苏林艺高 男，1946年，中国书画院教授，国家一级美术师。

润笔价格：4000~6000/平尺
供收藏家参考

Su Linyigao, born in 1946, is a National Class A artist and professor with China Painting and Calligraphy Academy.

Reference price: RMB4000-6000 per square feet

孙西原　1947年7月生，字道翁，山东邹城人，中国书法艺术研究院委员会会员。

润笔价格：2000~2500/平尺
供收藏家参考

孙西原
SUN XIYUAN

《南山十咏序》180*97　Foreword to Ode to Mount Nanshan 180*97

Sun Xiyuan, born in Zoucheng, Shandong Province, in July 1947 and with Daofeng as his literary name, is a member of the Committee of China Calligraphy Art Research Institute.

Reference price: RMB2000-2500 per square feet

张耀宗 ZHANG YAOZONG

大江东去浪淘尽千古风流人物故垒西边人道是三国周郎赤壁乱石穿空惊涛拍岸卷起千堆雪江山如画一时多少豪杰遥想公瑾当年小乔初嫁了雄姿英发羽扇纶巾笑谈间樯橹灰飞烟灭故国神游多情应笑我早生华发人生如梦一樽还酹江月

庚寅年作 苏轼词念奴娇赤壁怀古 耀宗

《苏轼词 念奴娇》180*97　Remembering Chibi by Su Dongpo 180*97

张耀宗 男，1939年生，中国书法家协会理事，华夏夕阳红书画艺术研究院名誉院长。

润笔价格：4000~5000/平尺
供收藏家参考

Zhang Yaozong, born in 1939, is a council member of China Calligraphers Association and Honorary President of China Xiyanghong Calligraphy and Painting Art Research Institute.

Reference price: RMB3000-4000 per square feet

赵庆显
ZHAO QINGXIAN

赵庆显 1951年生于河南，河南省书法家协会会员，中国三峡画院书法部主任，中国现代书画艺术研究院书法研究室主任。

润笔价格：5000~6000/平尺
供收藏家参考

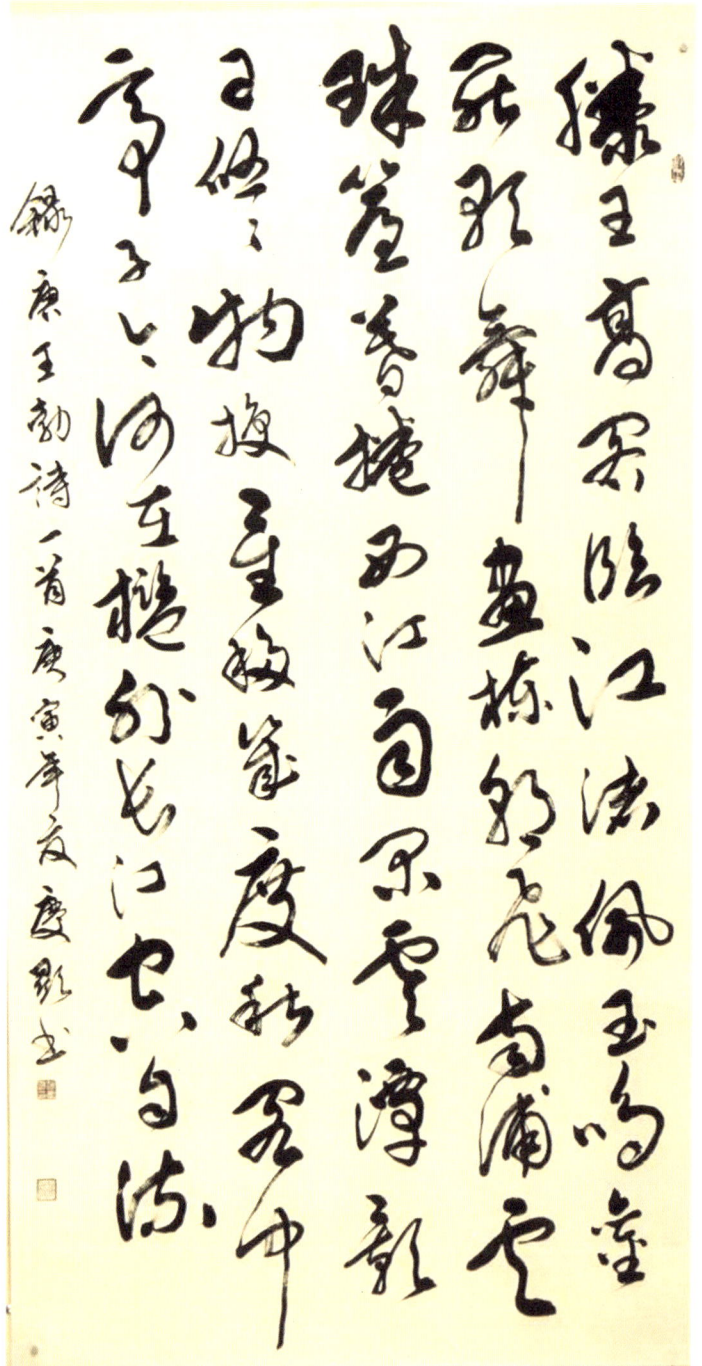

《王勃诗一首》 180*97　　*A Poem by Wang Bo 180*97*

Zhao Qingxian, born Henan in 1951, is a member of Henan Calligraphers Association, Director of Calligraphy Department of Three Gorges Art Gallery of China, and Director of Calligraphy Office of China Modern Calligraphy and Painting Research Institute.

Reference price: RMB5000-6000 per square feet

卞明华 1958年出生于江苏省江都市,中国收藏家协会会员,江苏省收藏家协会常务理事,江都市书协理事。

润笔价格:2000~3000/平尺
供收藏家参考

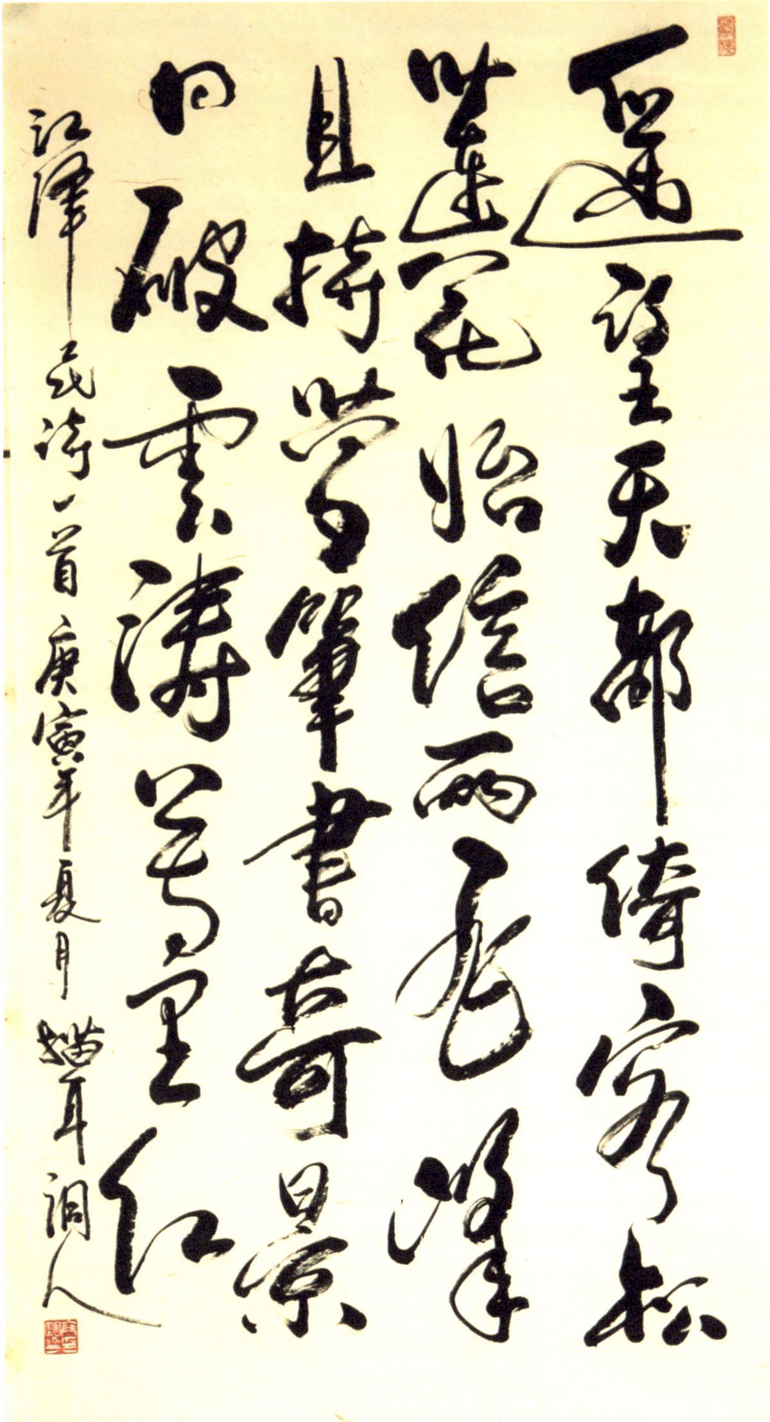

Bian Minghua, born in Jiangdu, Jiangsu Province, in 1958, is a member of China Association of Collectors, council member of Jiangsu Association of Collectors and of Jiangdu Calligraphers Association.

Reference price: RMB2000-3000 per square feet

《江泽民诗一首》 132*70   *A Poem by Jiang Zemin* 132*70

柴振福 CHAI MINGFU

柴振福 1966年生，中国书法家协会会员，河南省书画院特聘书法家。

润笔价格：5000~6000/平尺
供收藏家参考

Chai Mingfu, born in 1966, is a member of China Calligraphers Association and a calligrapher with Henan Calligraphy and Painting Academy.

Reference price: RMB3000-4000 per square feet

《鲁迅诗一首》180*96　　*A Poem by Lu Xun 180*96*

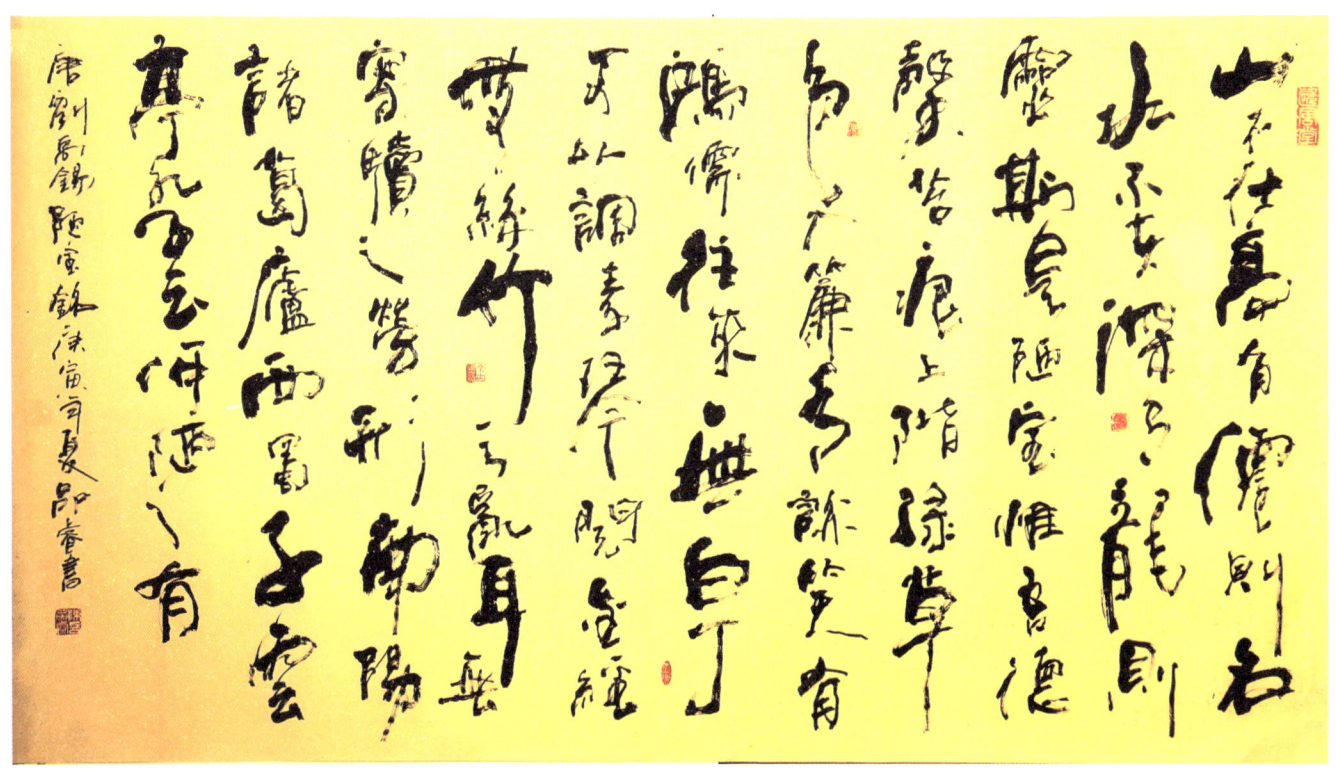

《刘禹锡 陋室铭》97*180　An Epigraph in Praise of My Humble Home by Liu Yuxi 97*180

陈克仁
CHEN KEREN

陈克仁,（陈品睿） 1951年生于湖南,中国艺术创作院理事,中国书法艺术家协会理事,湖南书法家协会会员。

润笔价格：3000~4000/平尺
供收藏家参考

Chen Keren (also known as Chen Pin Rui), born in Hunan Province in 1951, is a council member of China Art Creation Institute, of China Calligraphers Association, and member of Hunan Calligraphers Association.

Reference price: RMB3000-4000 per square feet

《横联》 97*180　　A Horizontal Couplet 97*180

冯　斌　FENG BIN

冯　斌　1938年生，当代华人书画艺术家，世界书画艺术名人。

润笔价格：3000~4000/平尺
供收藏家参

Feng Bin, born in 1938, is a contemporary Chinese calligrapher and painter and a world renowned artist.

Reference price: RMB3000-4000 per square feet

傅国强
FU GUOQIANG

傅国强 男，1965年生，现为中国书画家协会理事，中国书法家协会内蒙古分会会员。

润笔价格：2000~3000/平尺
供收藏家参考

《薛铸诗一首》96*180   A Poem by Xue Zhu 96*180

Fu Guoqiang, born in 1965, is a council member of China Calligrapher and Painter Association, and Inner Mongolia Branch of China Calligraphers Association.

Reference price: RMB2000-3000 per square feet

高菲
GAO FEI

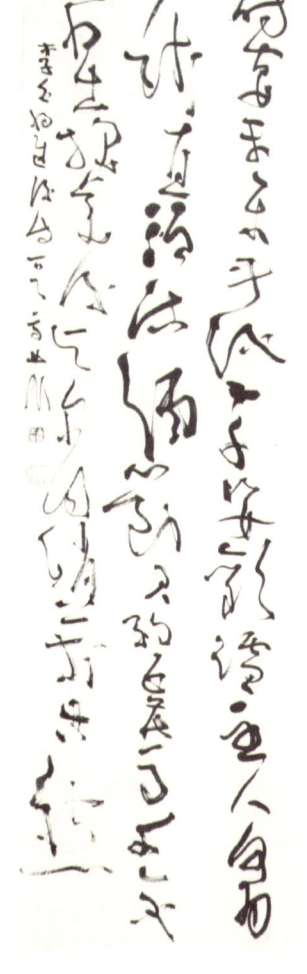
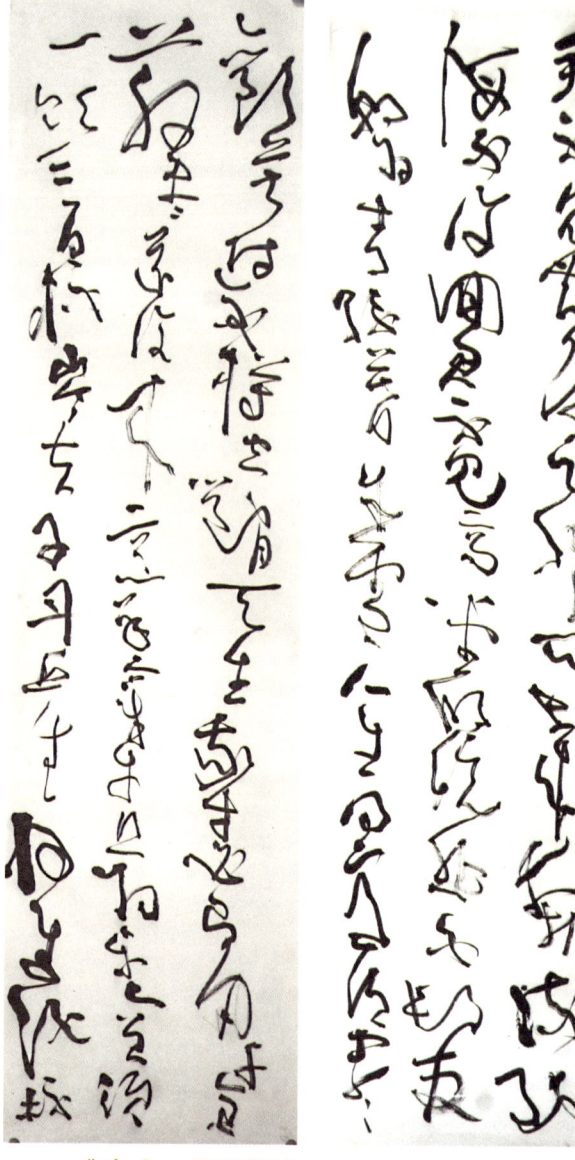

《李白 将进酒》 Bringing in the Wine by Li Bai

高　菲　山东烟台人，中国左笔书画家协会主席，中国扇子艺术协会理事，《人民艺术》报副理事长副主编，国际工商总会主席团主席兼左笔书法委员会主席。

润笔价格：5000~6000/平尺
供收藏家参考

Gao Fei, born in Yantai, Shandong Province, is President of China Association of Left-hand Calligraphy and Painting, council member of China Association of Fan Arts, Vice Council Director and Vice Editor in Chief of newspaper People's Art, and President of Left-hand Calligraphy Committee and of Presidium of International Federation of Commerce and Industry.

Reference price: RMB5000-6000 per square feet

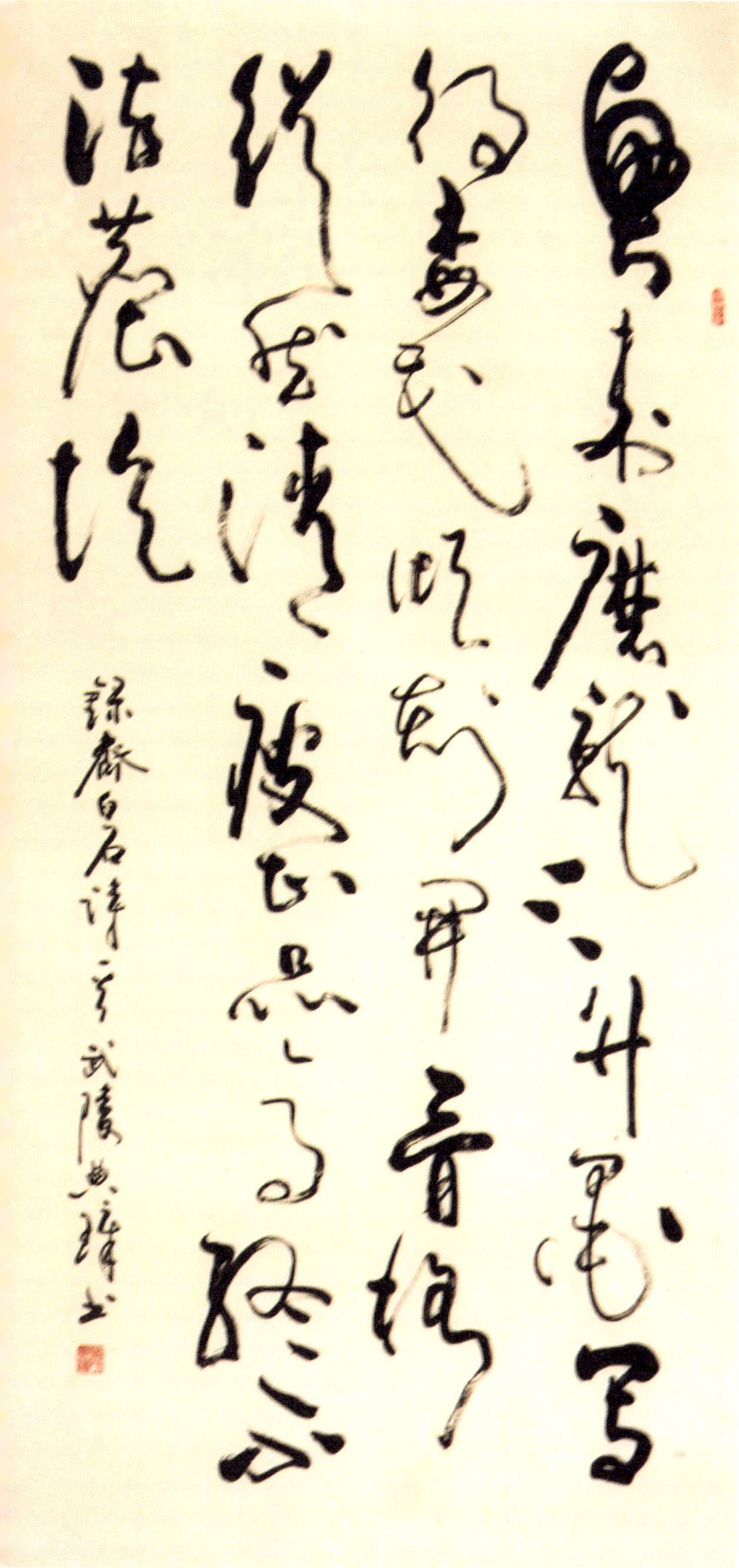

《齐白石诗一首》 *A Poem by Qi Baishi*

顾典璋
GU DIANZHANG

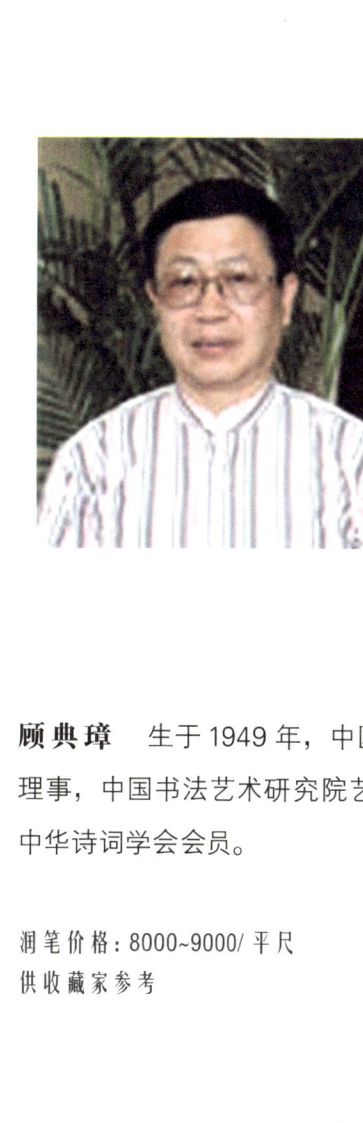

顾典璋 生于1949年，中国书画界联合会理事，中国书法艺术研究院艺术委员会委员，中华诗词学会会员。

润笔价格：8000~9000/平尺
供收藏家参考

Gu Dianzhang, born in 1949, is a council member of China Calligrapher and Painter Federation, member of Arts Committee of China Calligraphy Art Research Institute, and of Chinese Poetry Society.

Reference price: RMB8000-9000 per square feet

郝冰川
HAO BINGCHUAN

郝冰川 号，雲禅，一九五八年生于河南安阳，香港画院一级书画家，中国书画家学会会员。

润笔价格：4000~5000/平尺
供收藏家参考

Hao Bingchuan, with Yunchan as his literary name, born in Anyang, Henan Province in 1958, is a Class A calligrapher and painter with Hong Kong International Art Academy, and member of China Calligrapher and Painter Association.

Reference price: RMB4000-5000 per square feet

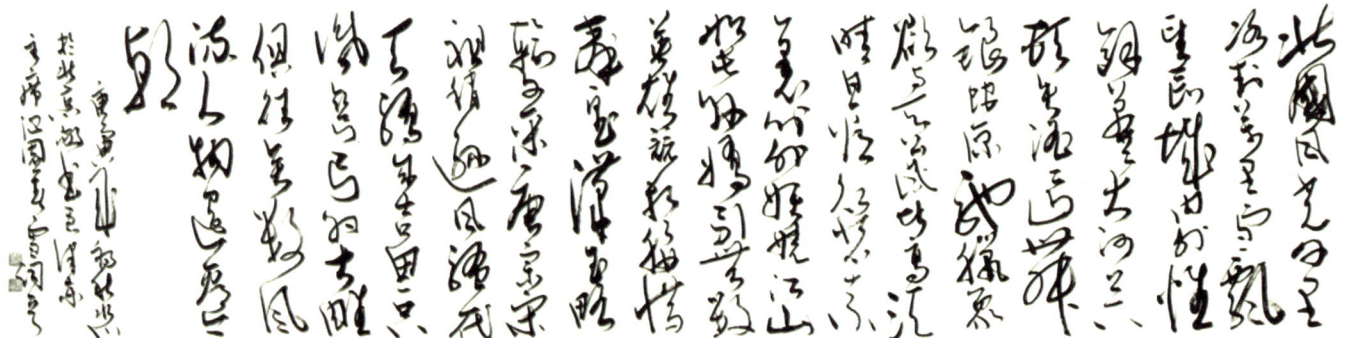

《毛主席词 沁园春雪》 *Snow by Mao Zedong*

郝志国 男，1944年生，中国美术家协会会员，中国版画家协会理事，大同大学美术教授，中国优秀版画家鲁迅奖获得者。

润笔价格：5000~6000/平尺
供收藏家参考

郝志国 HAO ZHIGUO

Hao Zhiguo, male, born in 1944, is a member of China Artists Association, council member of China Printmakers Association, fine art professor with Datong University, and winner of Lu Xun Prize for Excellent Printmakers in China.

Reference price: RMB5000-6000 per square feet

《行草条幅》180*97   A Scroll of Semi-cursive Script 180*97

侯炳茂 1936年生，北京丰台书法协会会员。

润笔价格：2000~3000/平尺
供收藏家参考

Hou Bingmao, born in 1936, is a member of Fengtai Calligraphers Association of Beijing.

Reference price: RMB2000-3000 per square feet

《楹联一副》206*68
*A Couplet 206*68*

焦宝成
JIAO BAOCHENG

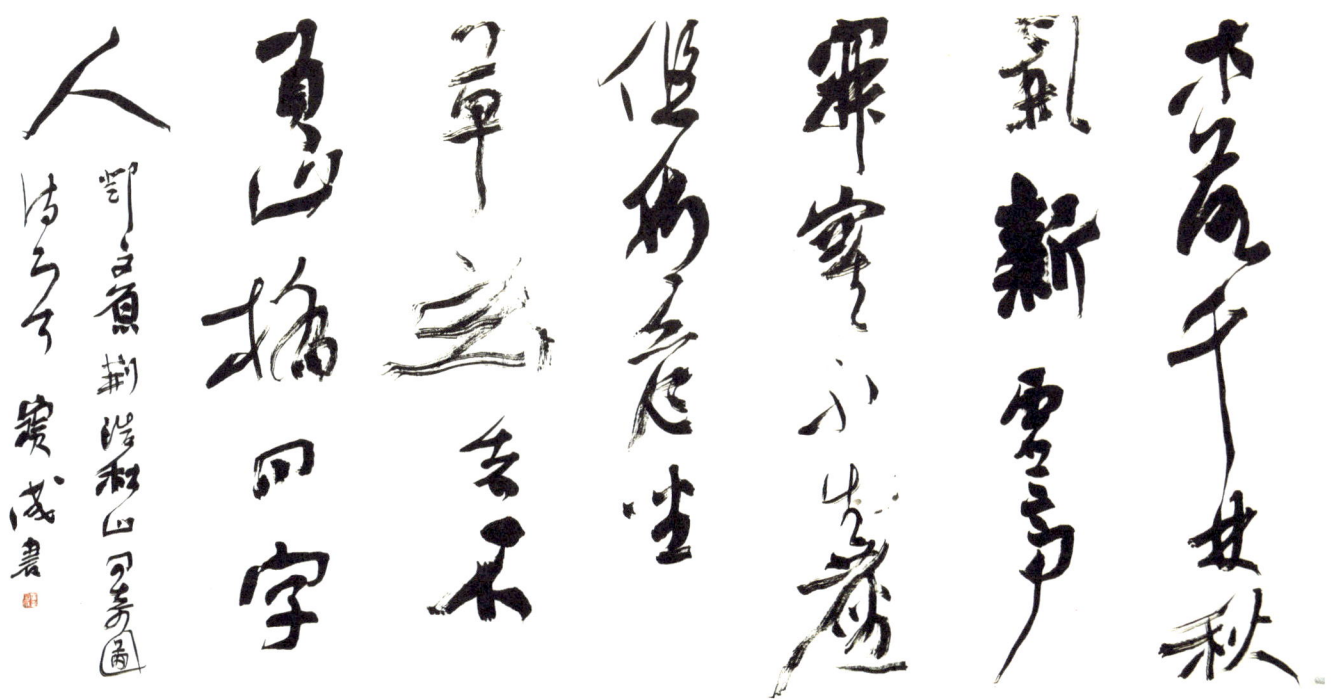

《行草横幅》97*180　A Scroll of Semi-cursive Script 97*180

焦宝成　男，1963年生，黑龙江省齐齐哈尔市书协副主席，中国书法家协会会员。

润笔价格：4000~5000/平尺
供收藏家参考

Jiao Baocheng, born in 1963, is Vice President of Qiqihar Calligraphers Associations in Heilongjiang Province, and member of China Calligraphers Association.

Reference price: RMB4000-5000 per square feet

李德杰 LI DEJIE

李德杰　北京京洲翰墨书画院副院长，北京华原书画院名誉院长，中国书画家协会会员。

润笔价格：3000~4000/平尺

供收藏家参考

Li Dejie is Vice President of Beijing Jingzhou Hanmo Calligraphy and Painting Gallery, Honorary President of Beijing Huayuan Calligraphy and Painting Gallery, and member of China Calligrapher and Painter Association.

Reference price: RMB3000-4000 per square feet

《古诗》180*97
An Ancient Poem 180*97

李廷干 1933年生，中国书画函授大学界首分校副教授，现代书法家，界首市、阜阳地区书法协会会员。

润笔价格：2000~3000/平尺
供收藏家参考

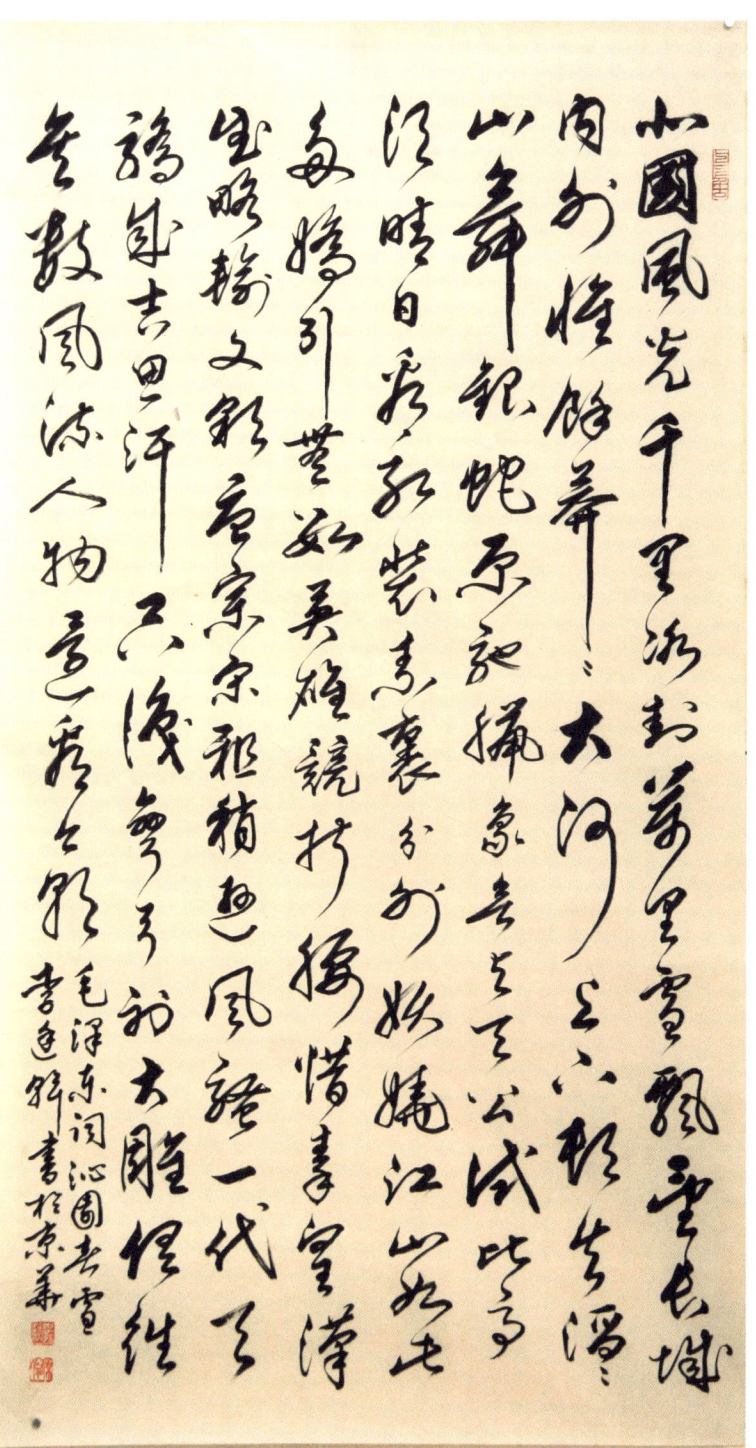

《毛泽东诗词》 180*97 *A poem by Mao Zedong 180*97*

Li Tinggan, born in 1933, is an assistant professor with Jieshou Branch of China Calligraphy and Painting Correspondence University, calligrapher, and member of Fuyang Calligraphers Association.

Reference price: RMB2000-3000 per square feet

《横幅》97*180 *A Horizontal Couplet 97*180*

李志刚
LI ZHIGANG

李志刚 中国书法家协会会员，省书法教育培训委员会理事。

润笔价格：4000~5000/平尺
供 收 藏 家 参 考

Li Zhigang is a member of China Calligraphers Association and council member of Provincial Calligraphy Education and Training Committee.

Reference price: RMB4000-5000 per square feet

林万华
LIN WANHUA

林万华 1969年出生，中国书法家协会会员，福清市政协委员，福清市书协副主席、美协理事。

润笔价格：3000~4000/平尺
供收藏家参考

Lin Wanhua, born in 1966, is a member of China Calligraphers Association, CPPCC member of Fuqing City, Vice President of Fuqing Calligraphers Association, and council member of Fuqing Artists Association.

Reference price: RMB3000-4000 per square feet

《道教经典》180*97　Taoist Classic 180*97

刘广源
LIU GUANGYUAN

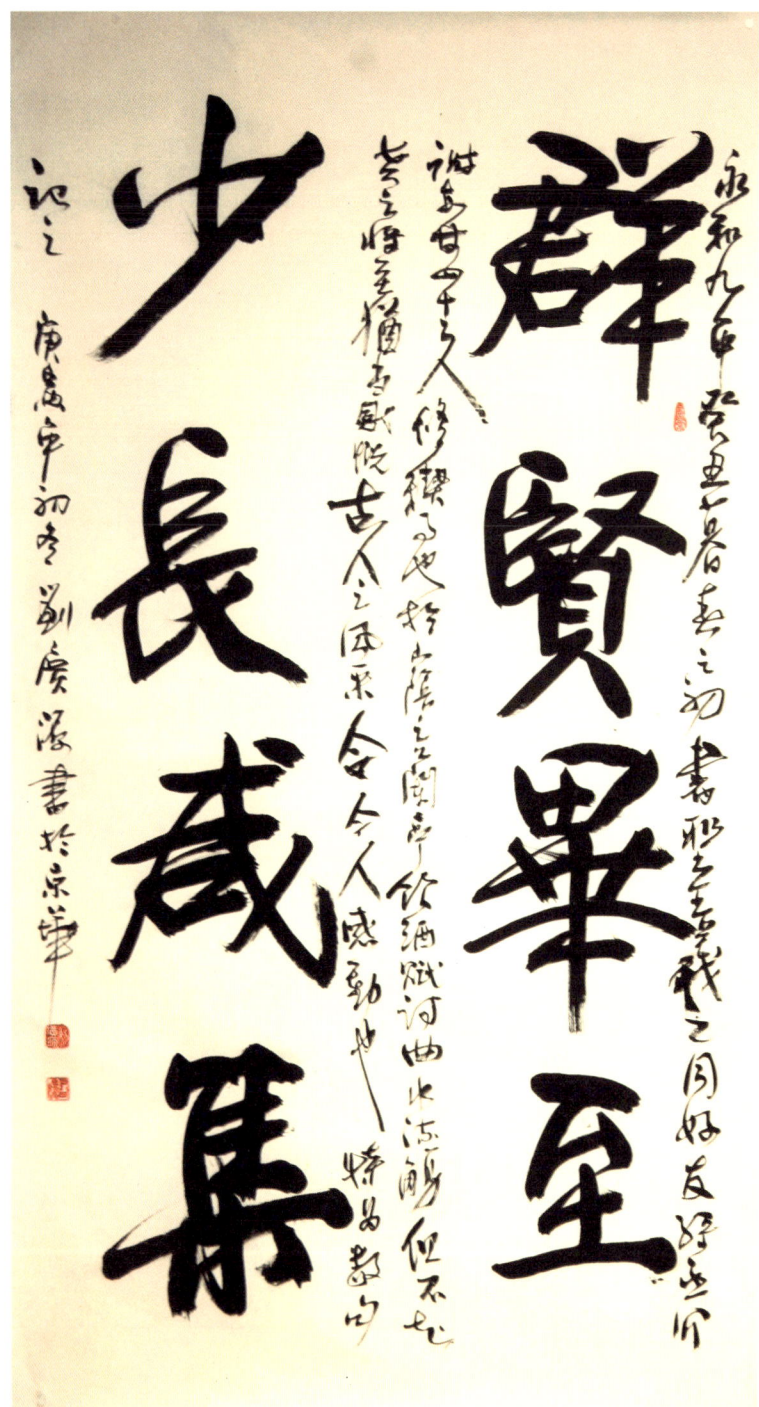

《楹联一副》 97*180 A Couplet 97*180

刘广源　1945年9月出生，中国书法家协会会员，武警书协副主席，中国国际书法研究会会员。

润笔价格：5000~6000/平尺
供收藏家参考

Liu Guangyuan, born in September 1945, is a member of China Calligraphers Association, Vice President of Armed Police Calligraphers Association, and member of China International Calligraphy Research Society.

Reference price: RMB5000-6000 per square feet

刘俊领
LIU JUNLING

刘俊领 男，1968年生，中国书画研究院会员，中山书画社，中国书法名家协会。

润笔价格：3000~4000/平尺
供收藏家参考

Liu Junling, born in 1968, is a member of China Calligrapher and Painter Association, of Sun Yat-sun Calligraphy and Painting Studio, and of China Association of Celebrity Calligraphers.

Reference price: RMB3000-4000 per square feet

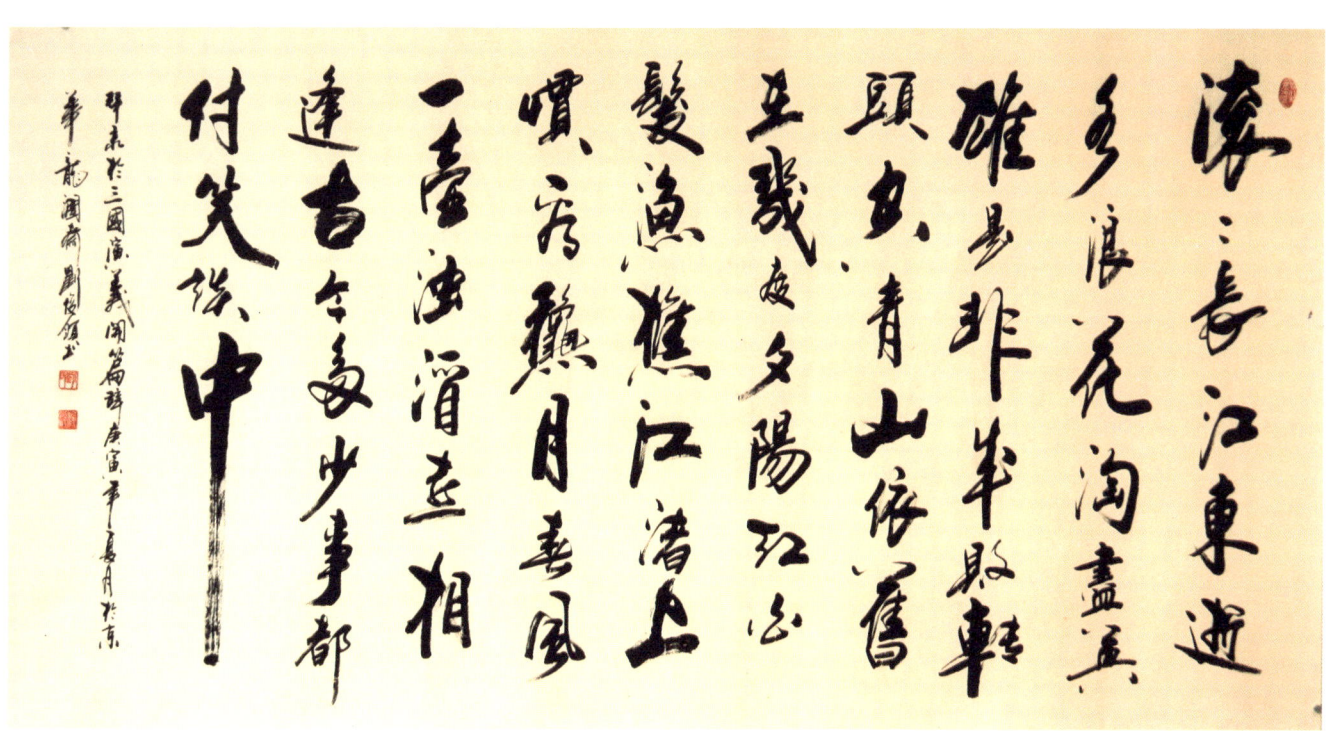

《三国演义开篇词》97*180　Opening Poem of Romance of Three Kingdoms　97*180

冯 力
FENG LI

冯 力 1971年生，河南省书法家协会会员，河南省群众艺术馆从事美术书法工作。

润笔价格：3000~4000/平尺
供收藏家参考

Feng Li, born in 1971, is a member of Henan Calligraphers Association and engages in fine arts and calligraphy-related work in Henan People's Museum.

Reference price: RMB3000-4000 per square feet

《登慈恩寺诗一首》 Ci'en Temple

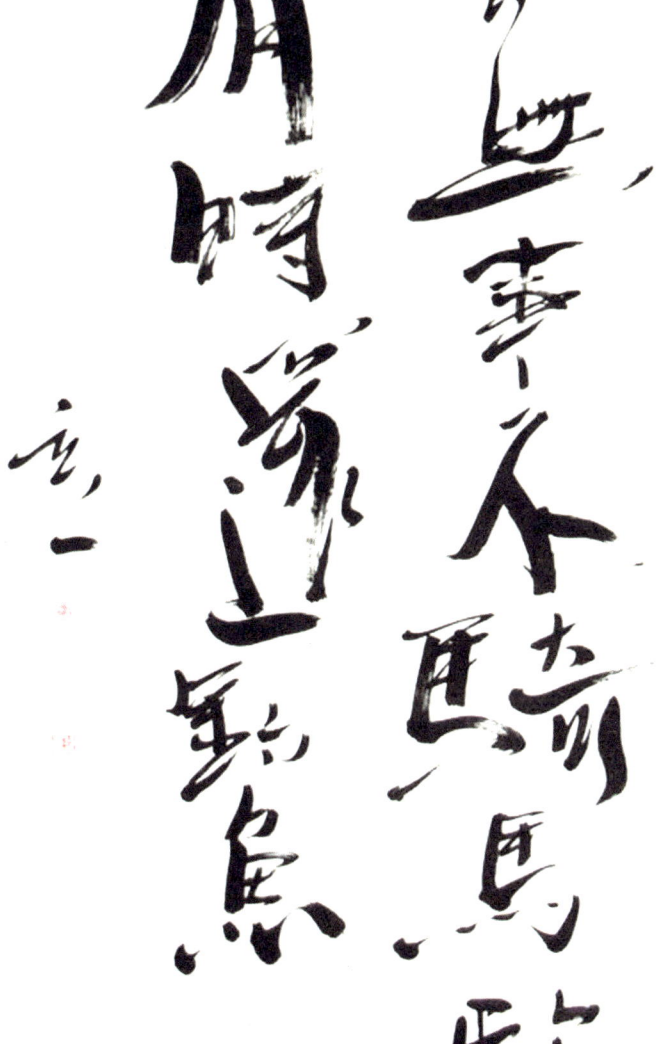

《条幅》 A Scroll

玄 一 国家级美术师，中国书画学会副主席，中国艺术家协会会员，中国玄体书法艺术研究院院长。

润笔价格：4000~5000/平尺
供收藏家参考

Xuan Yi, a state-level artist, is Vice President of China Calligrapher and Painter Association, member of China Artist Association, and President of China Metaphysical Calligraphy Art Research Institute.

Reference price: RMB4000-5000 per square feet

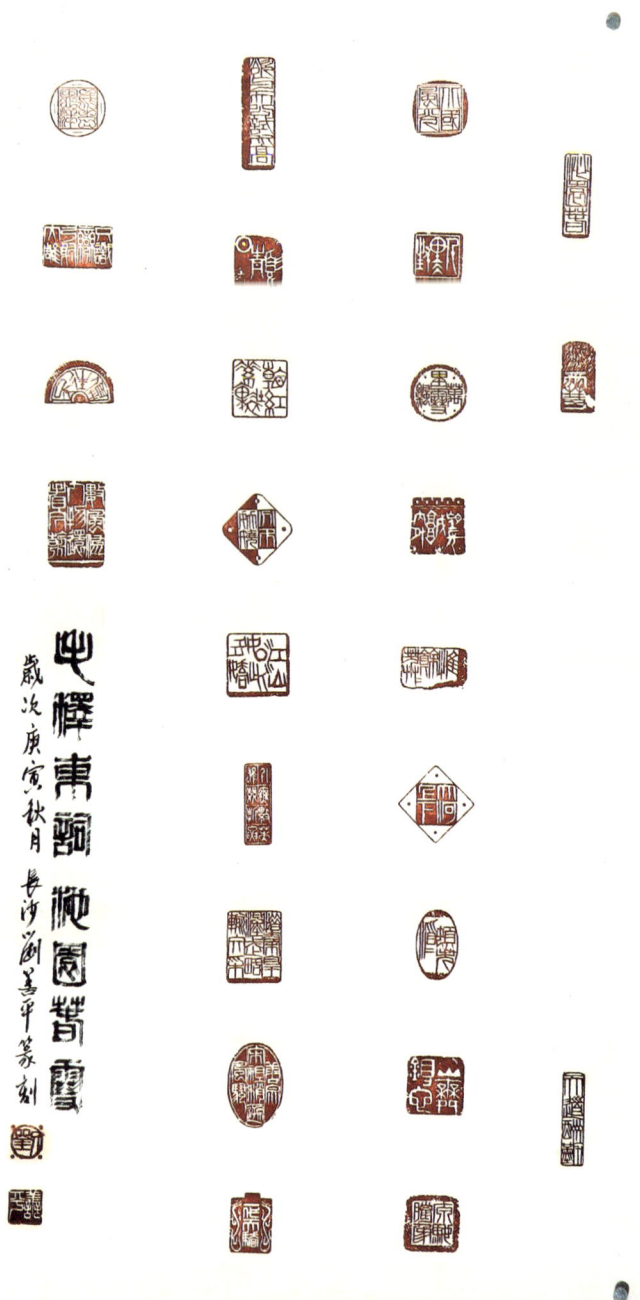

《篆刻》137*67 *Seal Cutting 137*67*

刘善平 男,高级工艺美术师,中国书画家协会理事,湖南省美术家协会会员。

润笔价格:每方 2000~3000
供收藏家参考

Liu Shanping is a senior industrial artist, council member of China Calligrapher and Painter Association, member of Hunan Artists Association.

Reference price: RMB2000-3000 per square feet

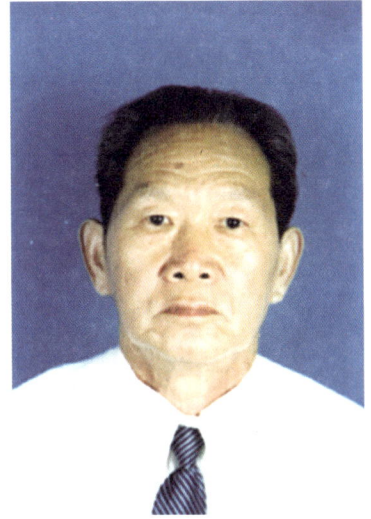

吕慧泉 男，1935年生，中国书法家学会会员，书法多次参加国际国内大展。

润笔价格：2000~3000/平尺
供收藏家参考

吕 慧 泉
LU HUIQUAN

Lu Huiquan, born in 1935, is a member of China Calligraphers Association whose works have been displayed at many international and domestic exhibitions.

Reference price: RMB2000-3000 per square feet

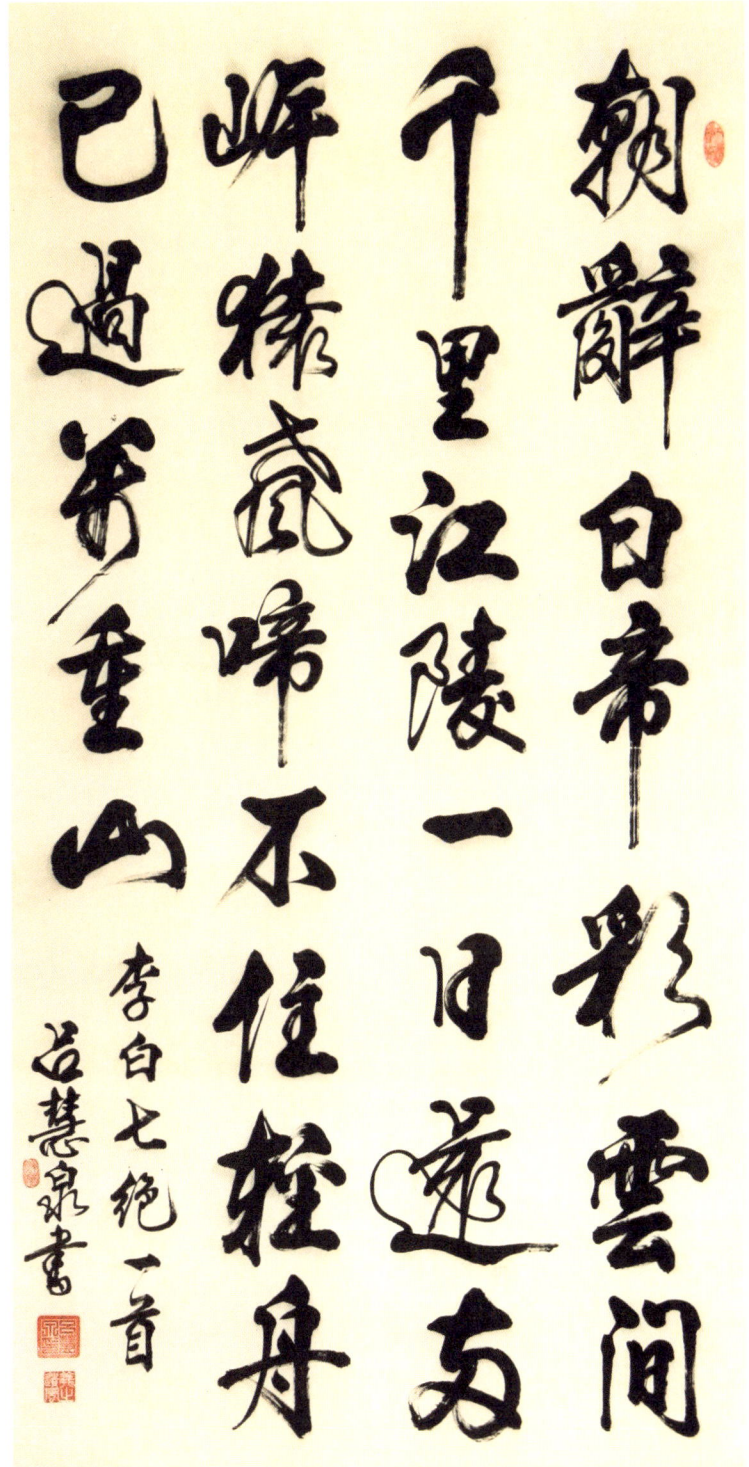

A Seven-character Quatrain by Li Bai
《李白七绝一首》

中国当代书画名家作品收藏指南 | 215

罗少模 男，号"山外人"，1946年生，现为四川省兴文县文物管理所所长，中国收藏家协会会员。

润笔价格：1500~2500/平尺
供收藏家参考

罗少模
LUO SHAOMO

Luo Shaomo, born in 1946, with Shanwairen as his literary name, is Director of Cultural Relic Management Office of Wenxian County in Sichuan Province and member of China Association of Collectors.

Reference price: RMB1500-2000 per square feet

《行草》180*97
*Semi-cursive Script 180*97*

马素常
MA SUCHANG

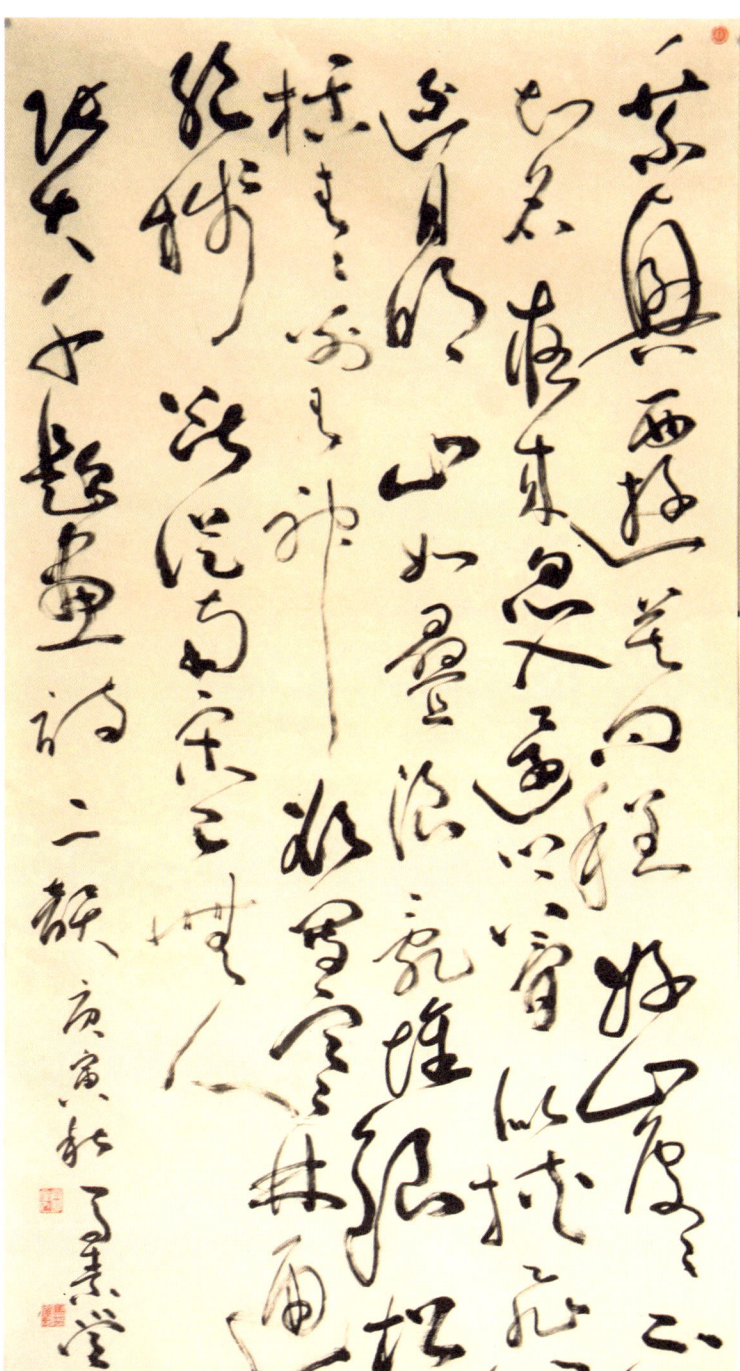

《张大千题画诗》 *A Poem by Zhang Daqian*

马素常（长） 1958年9月1日生，汉族，山东省章丘人，中国武陵书画家协会名誉主席，人民书画院特聘副院长，辽宁分会会员。

润笔价格：2000~3000/平尺
供收藏家参考

Ma Suchang, of Han nationality, born in Zhangqiu, Shandong Province, on September 1st, 1958, is Honorary President of China Wuling Association of Calligrapher and Painter, Vice President of People's Calligraphy and Painting Institute, and member of Liaoning Artists Association.

Reference price: RMB2000-3000 per square feet

《诸葛亮前出师表》96*180　First Memorial to King before Setting for War by Zhuge Liang 96*180

隋书粥
SUI SHUBI

隋书粥　1942年生，中国书画艺术家协会会员，山东省书法家协会会员，文登市书法协会顾问。

润笔价格：2500~3500/平尺
供收藏家参考

Sui Shubi, born in 1942, is a member of China Calligrapher and Painter Association, member of Shandong Calligraphers Association, and consultant of Wendeng Calligraphers Association.

Reference price: RMB2500-3500 per square feet

陶 然 原名陶宏畴，号了斋居士，中国书法家协会会员，新疆文史馆馆员。

润笔价格：5000~6000/平尺
供收藏家参考

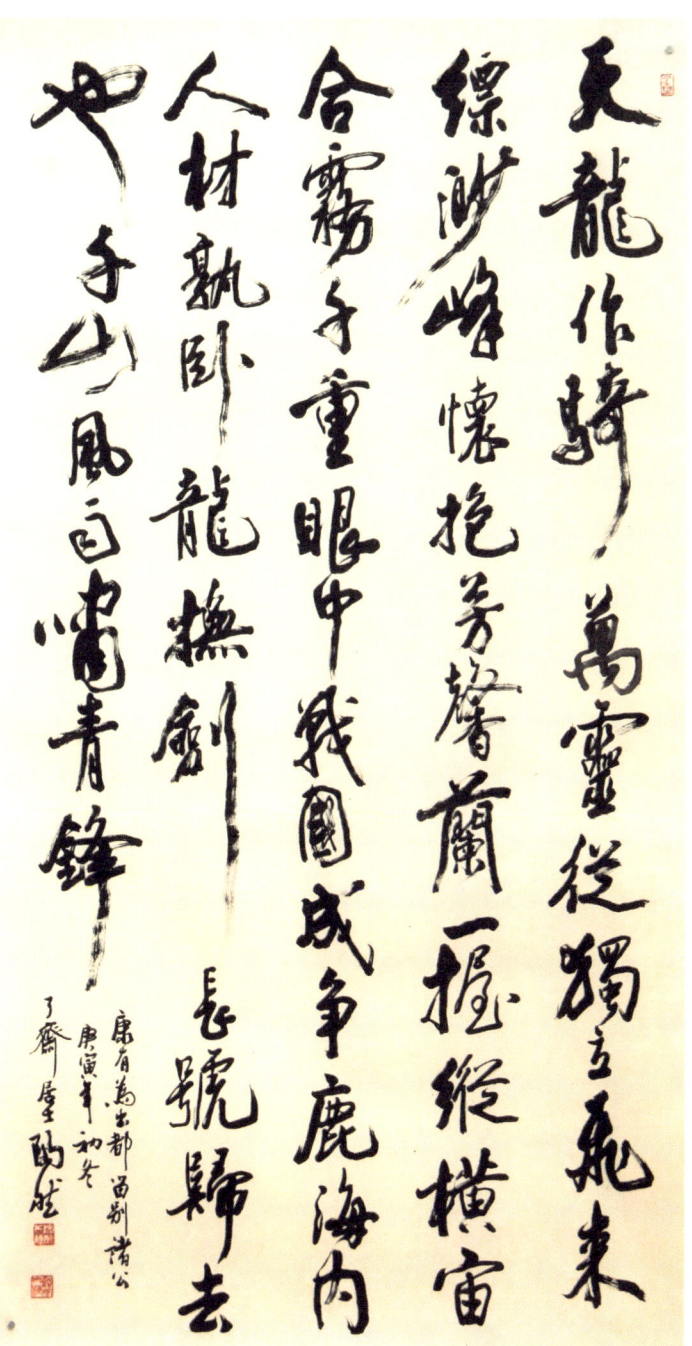

Tao Ran, previously known as Tao Hongchou and with Hermit of Liao Study as his literary name, is a member of China Calligraphers Association and works in Xinjiang Institute of Culture and History.

Reference price: RMB5000-6000 per square feet

《康有为诗一首》 180*97
*A Poem by Kang Youwei 180*97*

中国当代书画名家作品收藏指南

王虎江
WANG HUJIANG

王虎江 男 一九五二年生，北京市书法家协会会员，中国书法家协会会员。

润笔价格：3000~4000/平尺
供收藏家参考

Wang Hujiang, born in 1952, is a member of Beijing Calligraphers Association and of China Calligraphers Association.

Reference price: RMB3000-4000 per square feet

《三国演义开篇词》97*180　Opening Poem of Romance of Three Kingdoms 97*180

王 丽

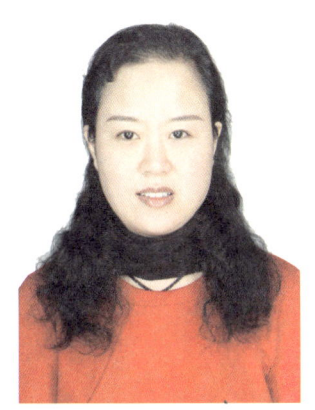

王　丽　1974年生，山东省书法家协会会员，济南市青年书法家协会会员。

润笔价格：2000~3000/平尺
供收藏家参考

Wang Li, born in 1974, is a member of Shandong Calligraphers Association and of Jinan Young Calligraphers Association.

Reference price: RMB2000-3000 per square feet

《庄子 秋水篇》200*73

Chapter of Autumn Water in Chuang Tzu 200*73

中国当代书画名家作品收藏指南

王文栋
WANG WENDONG

王文栋 1938年5月生,汉族,山东龙口人,一级美术师,山东省书法协会会员。

润笔价格:4000~5000/平尺
供收藏家参考

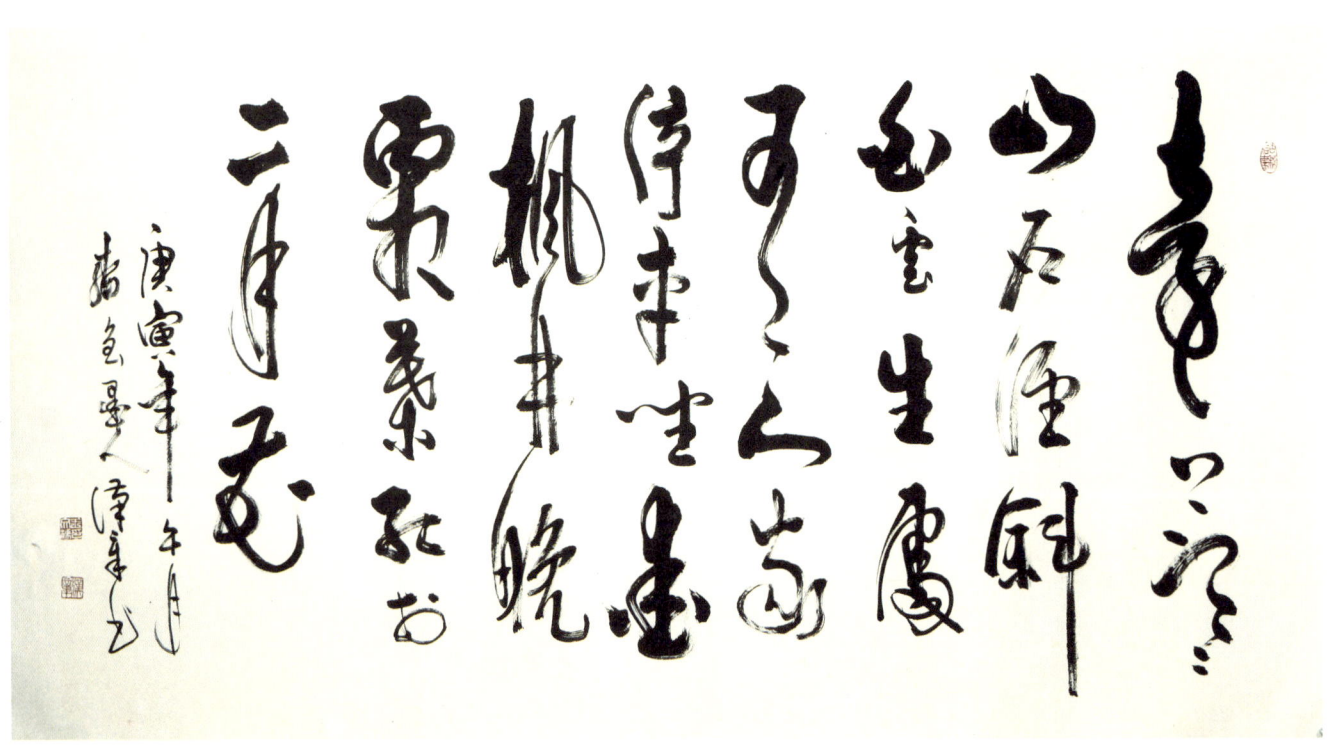

《古诗一首》 An Ancient Poem

Wang Wendong, of Han nationality, born in Longkou, Shandong Province, in May 1938, is a Class A artist and member of Shandong Calligraphers Association.

Reference price: RMB4000-5000 per square feet

萧 辉 Xiao Hui

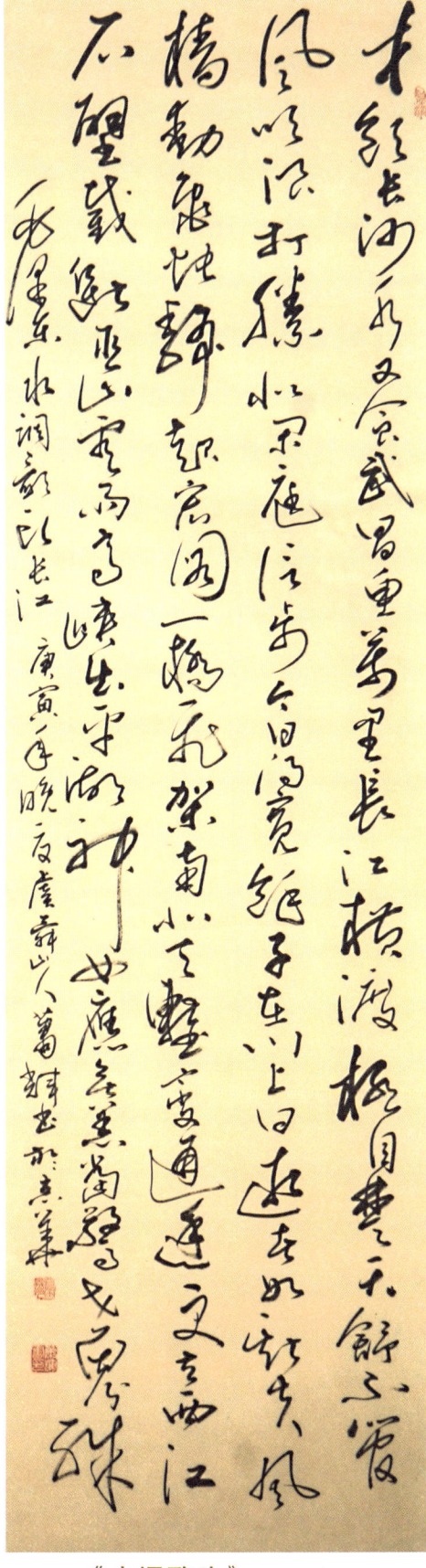

《水调歌头》 Swimming

萧 辉 1957年生，山西书法家协会会员，大唐书画院北京分院院长，中国书画艺术家协会理事。

润笔价格：5000~6000/平尺
供收藏家参考

Xiao Hui, born in 1957, is a member of Datong Calligraphers Association in Shanxi Province, President of Beijing Branch of Datang Calligraphy and Painting Gallery, and council member of China Association of Calligraphy and Painting Artists.

Reference price: RMB5000-6000 per square feet

熊安伟 XIONG ANWEI

熊安伟 1942年生，中国文人书协会员，中国国际文艺家协会会员。

润笔价格：2000~3000/平尺
供收藏家参考

Xiong Anwei, born in 1942, is a member of China Literary Calligraphers Association and of CIALA.

Reference price: RMB2000-3000 per square feet

《杜秋娘金缕衣》 *Gold-threaded Robe by Du Qiuniang*

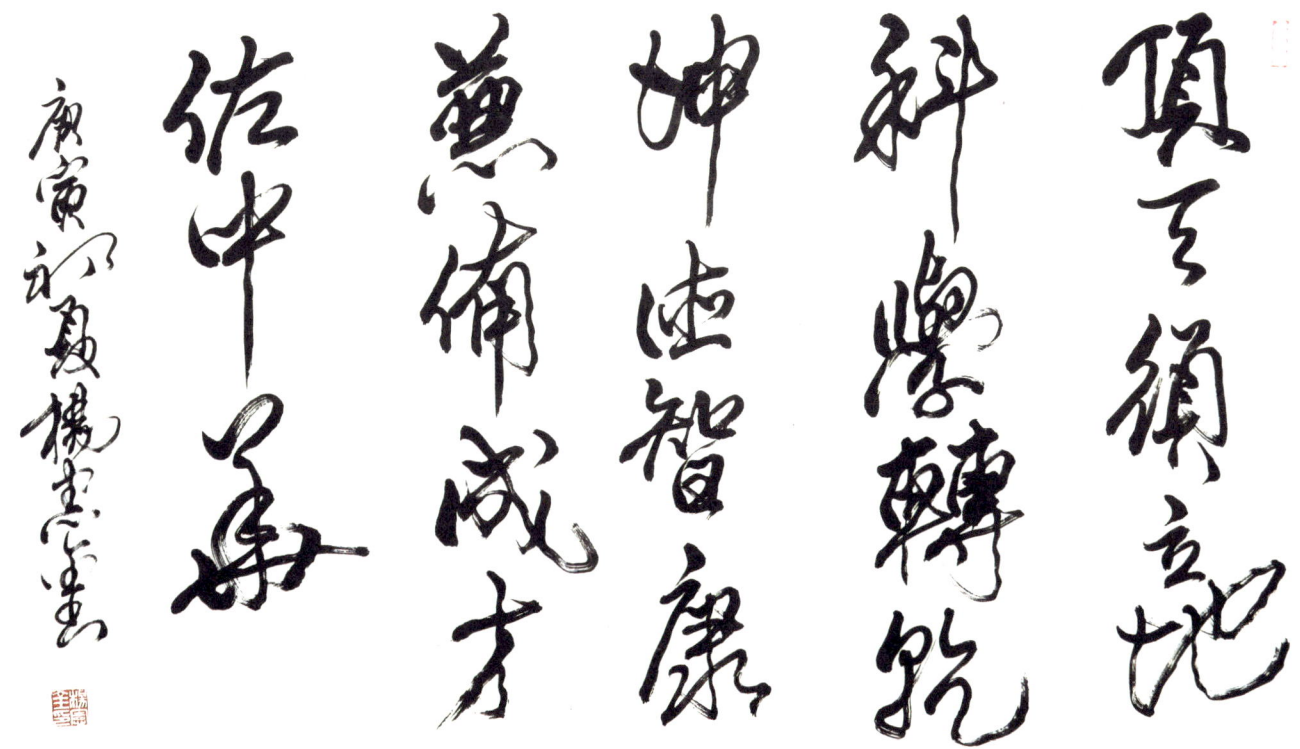

《行草》180*97 Semi-cursive Script 180*97

杨宪金
YANG XIANJIN

杨宪金 中国水墨艺术研究院院长,毛泽东书法艺术研究会副会长,中国楹联学会常务理事,中国楹联书法艺术委员会常务副主任,中国书法家协会会员。

润笔价格:9000~12000/平尺
供收藏家参考

Yang Xianjin is President of China Ink and Wash Art Research Institute, Vice President of Mao Zedong Calligraphy Art Research Society, standing council member of China Yinglian Society, standing Vice Director of Yinglian and Calligraphy Committee of China Yinglian Society, and member of China Calligraphers Association.

Reference price: RMB9000-12000 per square feet

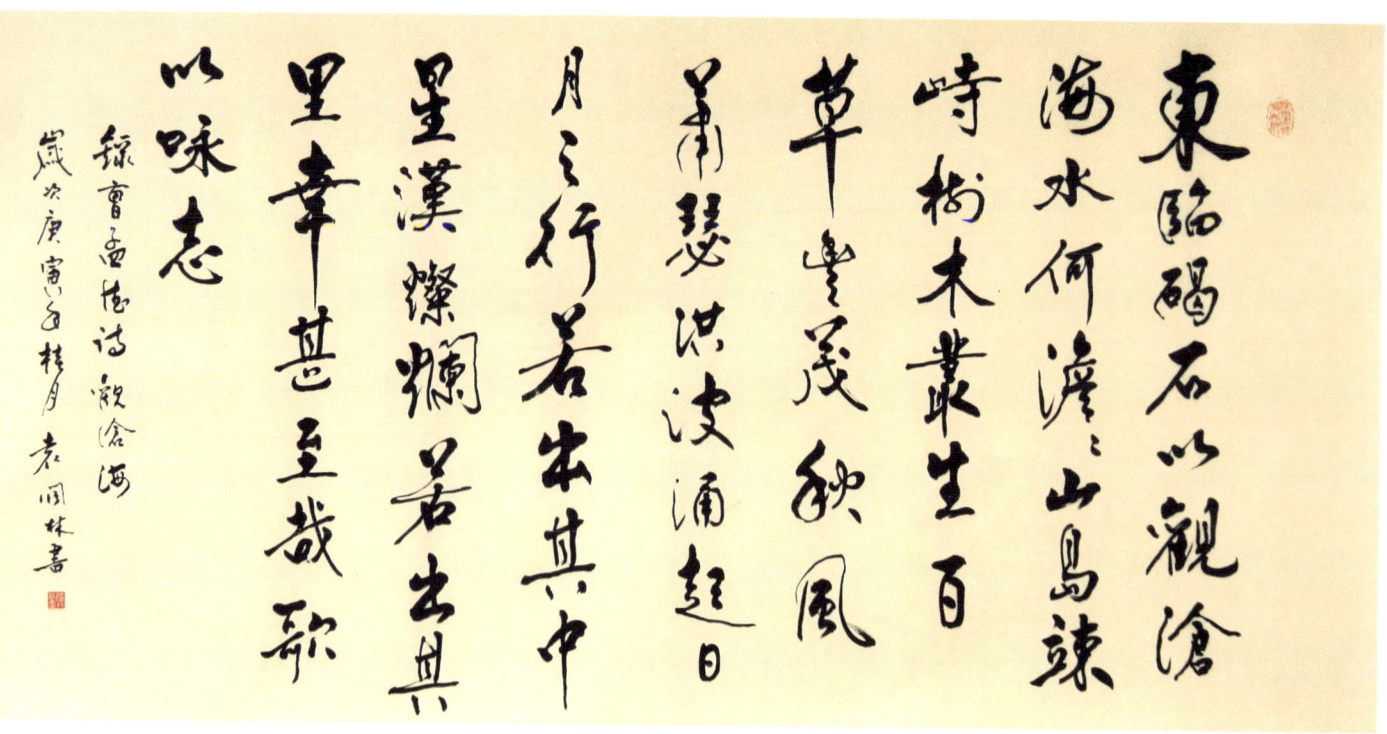

《观沧海》97*180　*The Sea 97*180*

袁阔林
YUAN KUOLIN

袁阔林　男、汉族、1940年生，山西省高平市人，中国书画艺术促进会，中国国际文艺家协会博学会员高级书法家，沈阳艺海拍卖代理中心特级书法家。

润笔价格：2000~3000/平尺
供收藏家参考

Yuan Kuolin, of Han nationality, born in Gaoping, Shanxi Province, in 1940, is a senior calligrapher of China Calligraphy and Painting Art Promotion Society and of CIALA and special-grade calligrapher of Shenyang Yihai Auction Center.

Reference price: RMB2000-3000 per square feet

岳英杰 YUAN KUOLIN

岳英杰 男，1957年出生，中国书画研究会会员，中国文化艺术发展促进会榜书协会会员，北京市残疾人书画会会员。

润笔价格：2000~3000/平尺
供收藏家参考

Yue Yingjie, born in 1957, is a member of China Calligraphy and Painting Research Association, member of Bangshu Committee of China Cultural and Art Promoting Society, and member of Beijing Disabled Artists Association.

Reference price: RMB2000-3000 per square feet

《刘禹锡陋室铭》 180*97
*An Epigraph in Praise of My Humble Home by Liu Yuxi 180*97*

翟玉龙
ZHAI YULONG

翟玉龙 字乐石，1960年生于北京，北京市师白研究会会员，书法家协会会员，美术家协会会员。

润笔价格：3000~4000/平尺
供收藏家参考

《观沧海》180*97 *The Sea 180*97*

Zhai Yulong, born in Beijing in 1960 and with Leshi as his literary name, is a member of Beijing Shibai Art Research Society, of Beijing Calligraphers Association and of Beijing Artists Association.

Reference price: RMB3000-4000 per square feet

张惠臣
ZHANG HUICHEN

张惠臣 1956年生人，中国书法家协会会员，刘炳森书画艺术研究院中心主任，中国北京书画院院长，中国名家书画院院士。

润笔价格：8000~10000/平尺
供收藏家参考

Zhang Huichen, born in 1956, is a member of China Calligraphers Association, Office Director of Liu Bingsen Calligraphy and Painting Art Research Institute, President of China Beijing Calligraphy and Painting Academy, and member of China Celebrity Calligraphy and Painting Gallery.

Reference price: RMB8000-10000 per square feet

《三国演义开篇词》70*236　Opening Poem of Romance of Three Kingdoms 70*236

《水调歌头》96*180 Swimming 96*180

赵子峰 男。1945年3月生于天津市蓟县，北京艺之瑰宝书画院高级书画师，北京宝延轩书画院院士，北京墨都书画院常务高级理事。

润笔价格：2000~3000/平尺
供收藏家参考

Zhao Zifeng, born in Jixian Couty, Tianjin, in March 1945, is a senior calligrapher and painter with Beijing Yizhi Guibao Calligraphy and Painting Gallery, member of Beijing Baoyanxuan Calligraphy and Painting Gallery, and senior standing council member of Beijing Modu Calligraphy and Painting Gallery.

Reference price: RMB2000-3000 per square feet

胡建雄
HU JIANXIONG

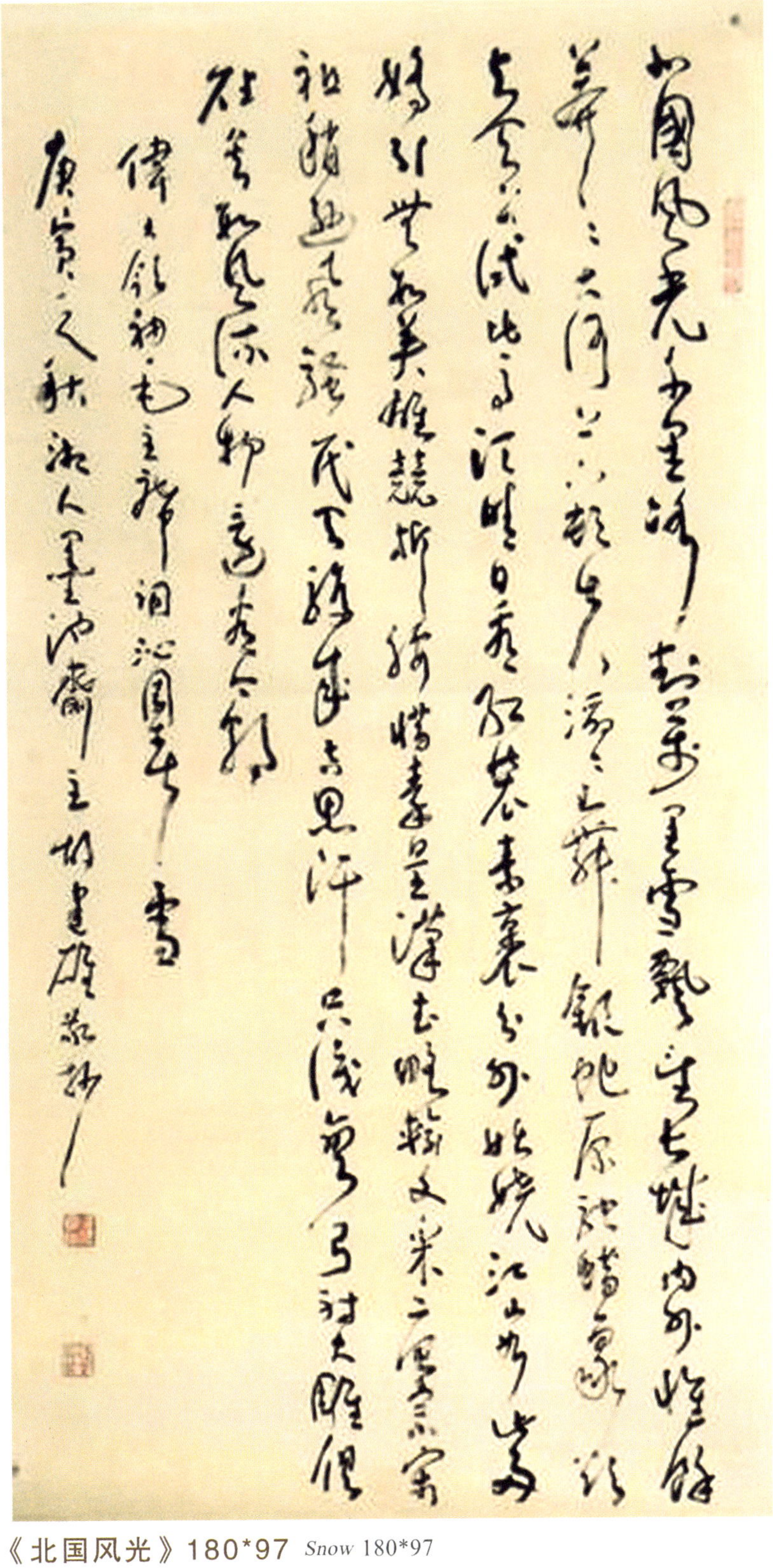

胡建雄　1954年生，解放军某部政委，中国书法家协会会员，中国收藏家协会会员。

润笔价格：8000~10000/平尺
供收藏家参考

Hu Jianxiong, born in 1954, a PLA political commissar, is a member of China Calligraphers Association and of China Association of Collectors.

Reference price: RMB8000-10000 per square feet

《北国风光》180*97　*Snow* 180*97

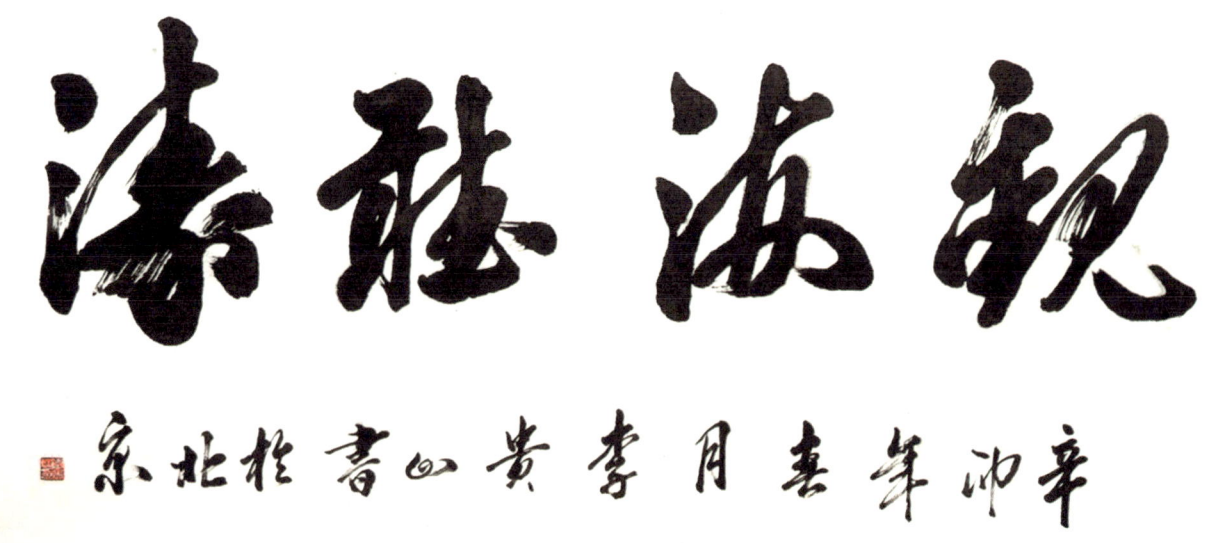

《观海听涛》 *Enjoying the Sea and Listening to the Tide*

李贵山
LI GUISHAN

李贵山 男,中国书法家协会理事,北京市建设文化艺术协会理事,北京昌平区书法家协会副主席。

润笔价格:5000~6000/平尺
供收藏家参考

Li Guishan is a council member of China Calligraphers Association and of Beijing Construction Culture and Art Association, and Vice President of Changping District Calligraphers Association in Beijing.

Reference price: RMB5000-6000 per square feet

墨 原
MO YUAN

墨原（汤禄仕） 1966年6月生于江苏扬州宝应，中国书法家协会会员，中国"扬州八怪"遗风继承与创新者，江苏省国画院特聘书法家。

润笔价格：5000~6000/平尺
供收藏家参考

Mo Yuan (Tang Lushi), born in June 1966 in Baoying, Yangzhou, Jiangsu Province, is a member of China Calligraphers Association and distinguished calligrapher Jiangsu Chinese Painting Institute who have inherited and made innovations to the art of Eight Eccentrics of Yangzhou.

Reference price: RMB5000-6000 per square feet

《念娇奴 赤壁怀古》 *Remembering Chibi*

冯志福 FENG ZHIFU

冯志福 一九四四年一月生，中国书法家协会理事，河南省书法家协会副主席，副研究馆员，《陆游诗一首》。

润笔价格：6000~8000/平尺
供收藏家参考

Feng Zhifu, born in January 1944, is a council member of China Calligraphers Association, Vice President of Henan Calligraphers Association, and assistant librarian.

Reference price: RMB6000-8000 per square feet

《陆游诗一首》 *A Poem by Lu You*

王若木 WANG RUOMU

山光物態弄春暉,莫為輕陰便擬歸。縱使晴明無雨色,入雲深處亦沾衣。

錄唐朝張旭詩山中留客 乙酉年庚月於古城長安硯農齋 王若木

《古诗一首》 An Ancient Poem

王若木 字拂日,号砚农斋主,生于陕西长安,西安市书法家协会理事,陕西省书法家协会会员。

润笔价格:3000~4000/平尺
供收藏家参考

Wang Ruomu, with Furi and Master of Yannong Study as his literary names, and born in Xi'an, is a council member of Xi'an Calligraphers Association and member of Shaanxi Calligraphers Association.

Reference price: RMB3000-4000 per square feet

《杜牧诗一首》
A Poem by Du Mu

邢　秀　国家一级美术师，中国书法家协会会员，内蒙古书法家协会副主席，巴彦淖尔市书协主席。

润笔价格：5000~6000/平尺
供收藏家参考

Xing Xiu, a National Class A artist, is a member of China Calligraphers Association, Vice President of Inner Mongolia Calligraphers Association, and President of Bayannur Calligraphers Association.

Reference price: RMB5000-6000 per square feet

《观天象》69*138 Examining Celestial Phenomena 69*138

姚 诚
YAO CHENG

姚　诚　1964年，广东电视台编导，市书协会员。

润笔价格：2000~3000/平尺
供收藏家参考

Yao Cheng, born in 1964, is a producer-director of Guangdong TV Station and member of a municipal calligraphers association.

Reference price: RMB2000-3000 per square feet

张际春　1948年11月出生于许昌，河南省安阳市人，中国书法家协会会员，河南省书法家协会学术委员会委员，新乡市书法家协会副主席，新乡市书画学会副会长。

润笔价格：5000~6000/平尺
供收藏家参考

张际春
ZHANG JICHUN

Zhang Jichun, born in Xuchang in November 1948, is a native of Anyang, Henan Province. He is a member of China Calligraphers Association, Member of Academic Committee of Henan Calligraphers Association, and Vice President of Xinxiang Calligraphers Association and of Xinxiang Calligrapher and Painter Association.

Reference price: RMB5000-6000 per square feet

《邓石如长联》

A Long Couplet by Deng Shiru

张复元 ZHANG FUYUAN

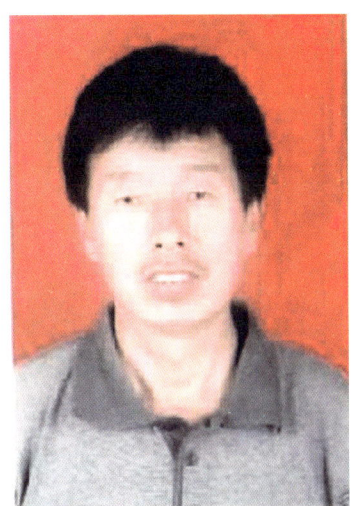

张复元 男，1958年生，沛县政协书协联合会员。

润笔价格：2000~3000/平尺
供收藏家参考

Zhang Fuyuan, born in 1958, is a CPPCC member and a member of Calligraphers Association of Peixian County.

Reference price: RMB2000-3000 per square feet

《千字文》 190*80
1000 Character Classic 190*80

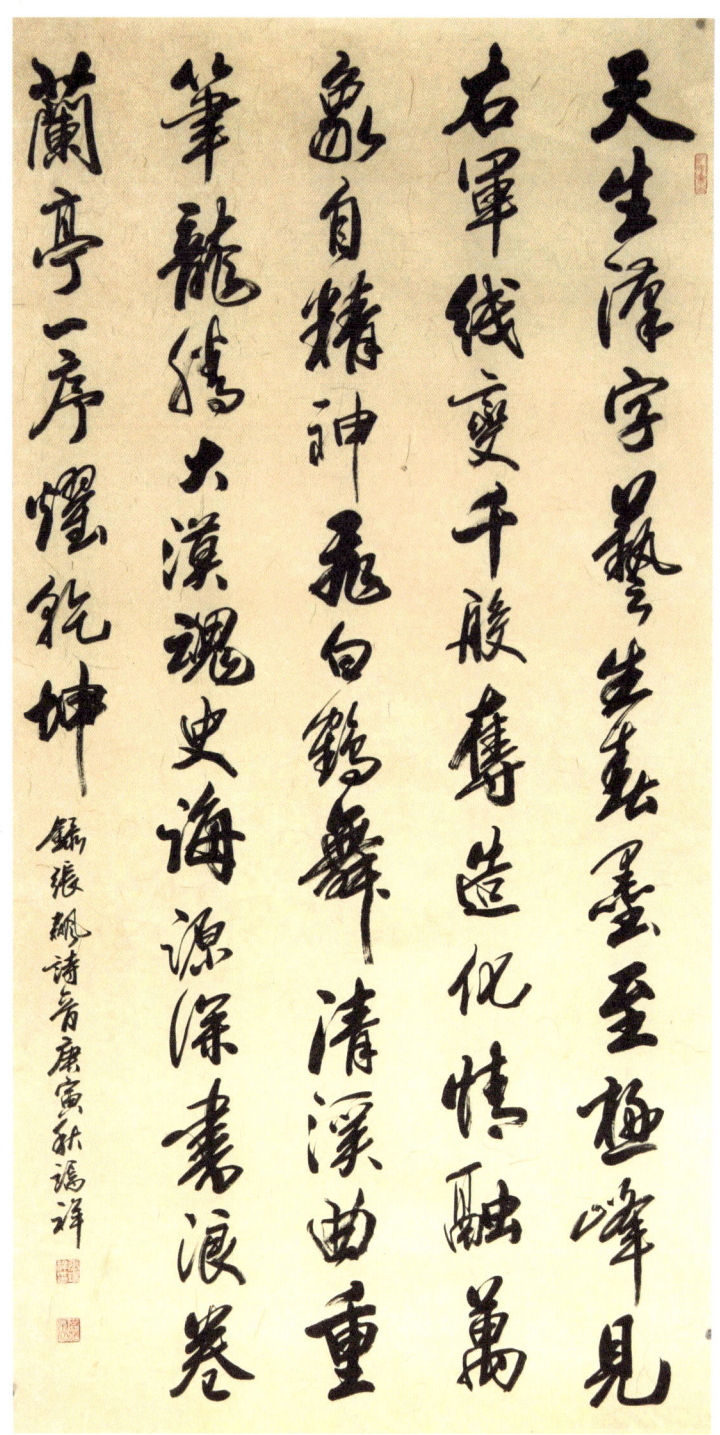

《张飙诗一首》 A Poem by Zhang Biao

张瑞祥
ZHANG RUIXIANG

张瑞祥 男，1955年生，中共中央直属机关书画协会常务理事，副秘书长，中国人才研究会艺术家学部委员会常务理事，副秘书长，中国书法艺术家协会理事，北京市西城区文联理事。

润笔价格：8000~10000/平尺
供收藏家参考

Zhang Ruixiang, born in 1955, is a standing council member and Vice Secretary General of Calligrapher and Painter Association of Organs Directly under the Central Committee of the CPC, standing council member and Vice Secretary General of Artists Committee of China Talents Society, council member of China Calligraphers Association, and council member of Xicheng District Federation of Literary and Art Circles.

Reference price: RMB8000-10000 per square feet

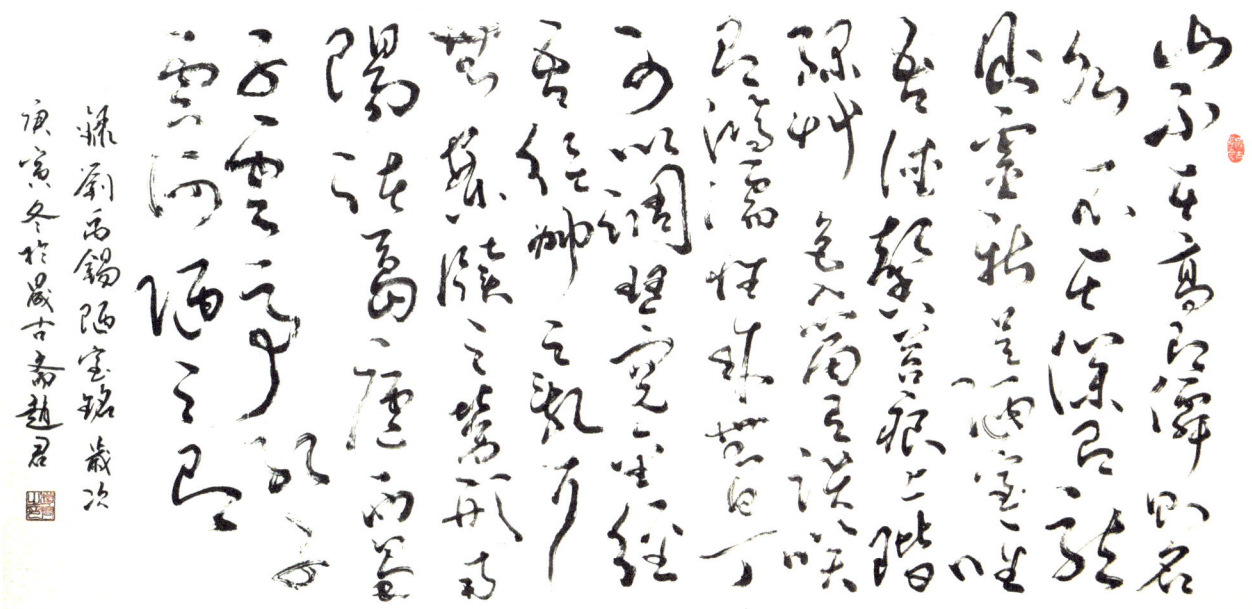

《陋室铭》 An Epigraph in Praise of My Humble Home

赵 君 1951年生，中国书画研究会副秘书长，劳动人事部艺术品鉴定师。

润笔价格：3000~4000/平尺
供收藏家参考

Zhao Jun, born in 1951, is Vice Secretary General of China Calligraphy and Painting Research Society and Art Ware Assessor of Ministry of Human Resources and Social Security.

Reference price: RMB3000-4000 per square feet

王乃勇
WANG NAIYONG

王乃勇 1969年2月生，国家二级美术师，中国书法家协会会员，中国书协培训中心教授，河南省书法家协会理事，行书专业委员会付主任。

润笔价格：5000~6000/平尺
供收藏家参考

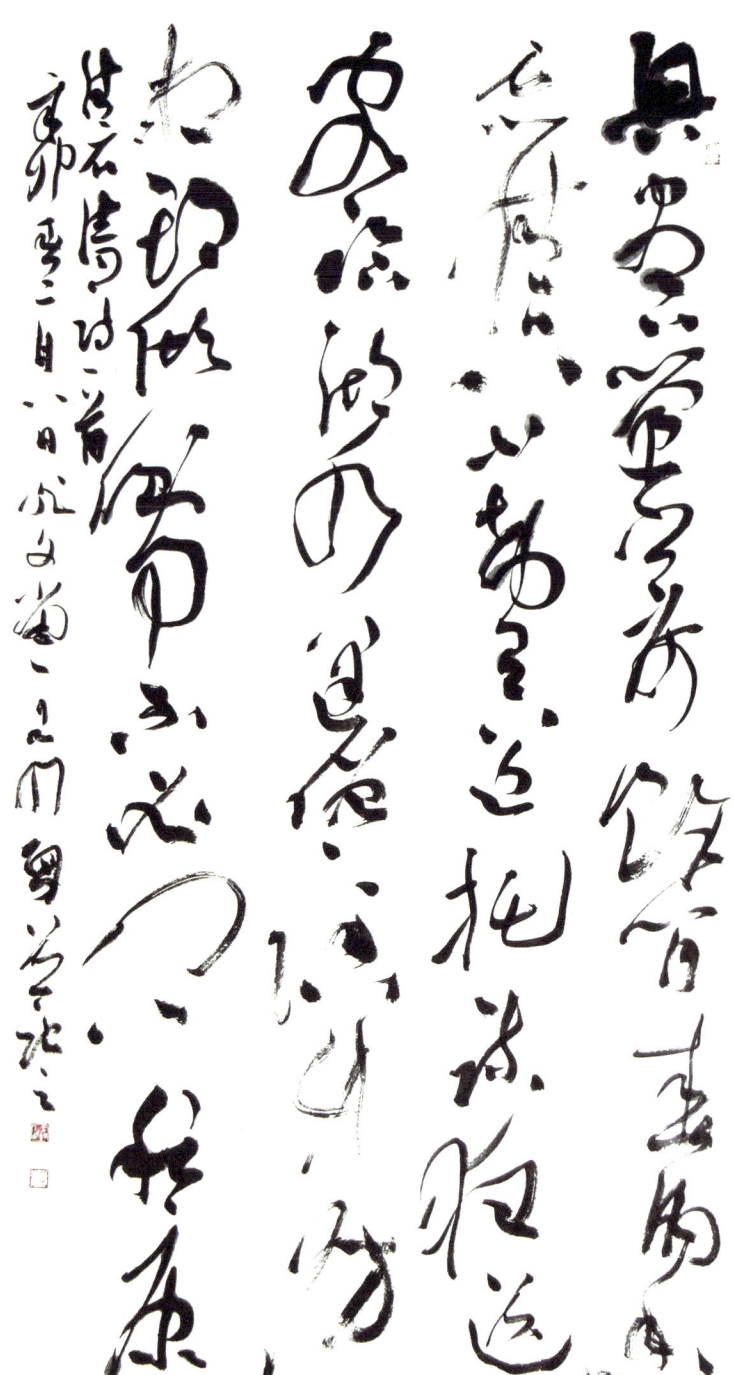

《石涛诗一首》 A Poem by Shi Tao

Wang Naiyong, a National Class B artist born in February 1969, is a member of China Calligraphers Association and professor with Training Center of CCA. He is also a council member of Henan Calligraphers Association and Vice Director of Semi-cursive Committee of HCA.

Reference price: RMB5000-6000 per square feet

赵志辉
ZHAO ZHIHUI

赵志辉 1955年生，男，汉族，研究生学历，中国书法家协会会员，中国军事写作协会副会长兼秘书长。

润笔价格：8000~10000/平尺
供收藏家参考

Zhao Zhihui, born in 1955, of Han nationality, and a Master's degree holder, is a member of China Calligraphers Association and Vice President as well as Secretary General of China Military Writers Association.

Reference price: RMB8000-10000 per square feet

《观沧海》 *The Sea*

周继中 ZHOU JIZHONG

周继中（阿中） 1971年生，中国书法家协会会员，巢湖市书法家协会理事，巢湖市硬笔书法家协会常务副主席，含山县书法家协会副主席，香港书法家协会会员。

润笔价格：5000~6000/平尺
供收藏家参考

Zhou Jizhong (also A Zhong), born in 1971, is a member of China Calligraphers Association, council member of Chaohu Calligraphers Association, standing Vice President of Chaohu Association of Pen Calligraphers, Vice President of Hanshan County Calligraphers Association, and member of Hong Kong Calligraphers Association.

Reference price: RMB4000-5000 per square feet

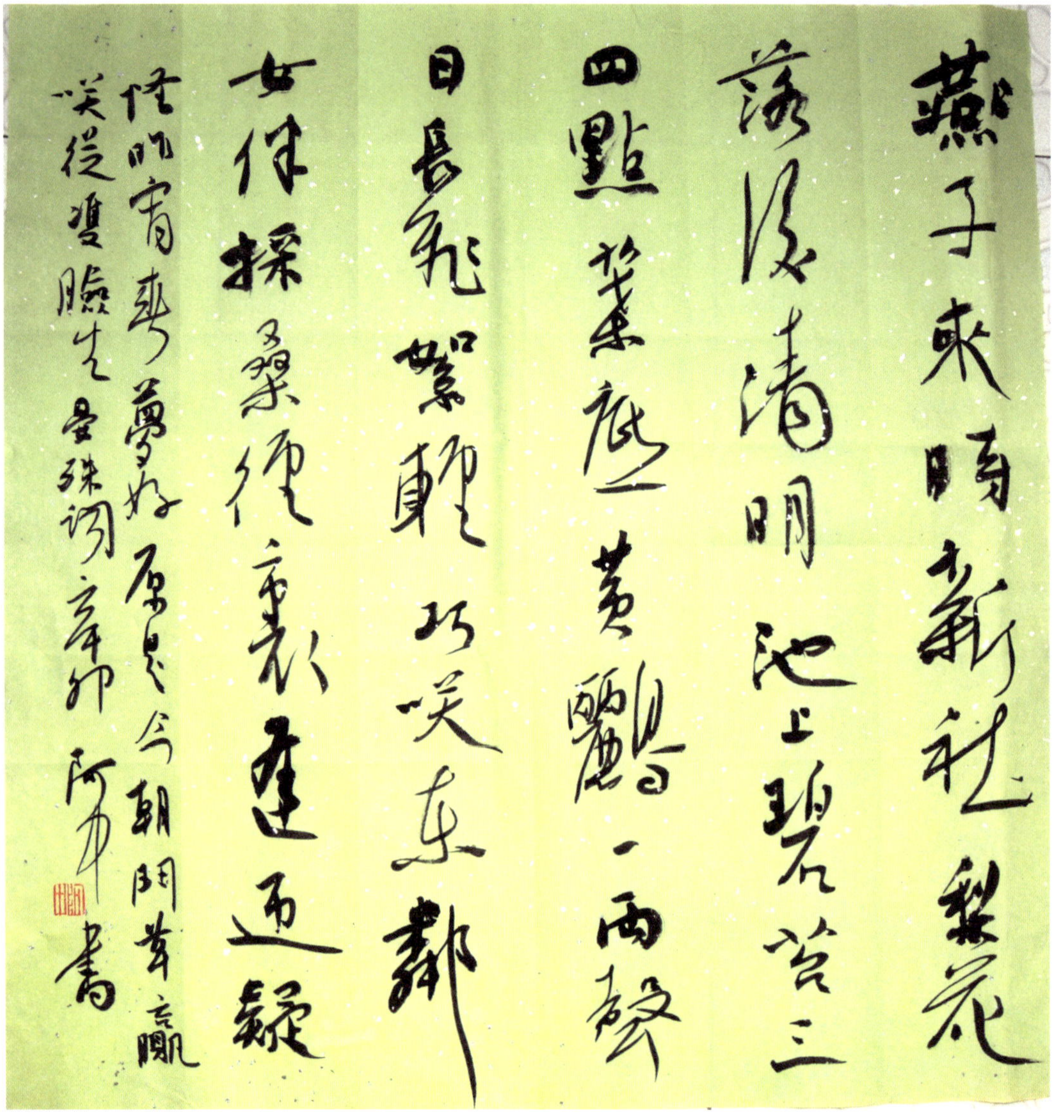

《晏殊词》
A Poem by Yan Shu

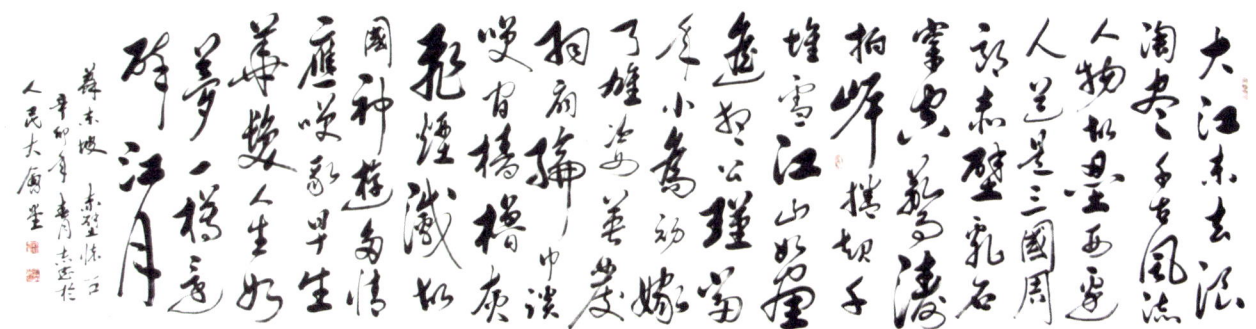

《苏东坡赤壁怀古》 Remembering Chibi by Su Dongpo

蒋志忠
JIANG ZHIZHONG

蒋志忠 男，1943年生，中国和合画院副院长，中国书画家协会理事，海峡两岸交流协会理事。

润笔价格：4000~5000/平尺
供收藏家参考

Jiang Zhizhong, born in 1943, is Vice President of China Hehe Painting Gallery, council member of China Calligrapher and Painter Association, and member of Cross Straights Exchange Association.

Reference price: RMB4000-5000 per square feet

陈 祥
CHEN XIANG

陈 祥　1949年12月生于武汉，1983年加入武汉书法家协会，国家一级书画师，深圳半岛书画会艺术顾问，香港国际书画家交流协会秘书长。

润笔价格：2000~3000/平尺
供收藏家参考

Chen Xiang, born in Wuhan in December 1949, joined Wuhan Calligraphers Association in 1983.
He is now a National Class A artist, art consultant of Shenzhen Peninsula Calligraphy and Painting Association, and Secretary General of Hong Kong International Calligraphy and Painting Exchange Association.

Reference price: RMB2000-3000 per square feet

《对联》
A Couplet

张天文
ZHANG TIANW

张天文 男，1953年生，中国书画家协会常务理事，中国书法学会理事，国防大学耕砚堂书画院艺术顾问，北京长城书画院常务副院长

润笔价格：5000~6000/平尺。
供收藏家参考

Zhang Tianwen, male, born in 1953, is a standing council member of China Calligrapher and Painter Association, council member of China Calligraphers Association, art consultant of Gengyan Hall Calligraphy and Painting Academy of National University of Defense Technology, and Vice President of Beijing Great Wall Calligraphy and Painting Gallery.

Reference price: RMB5000-6000 per square feet

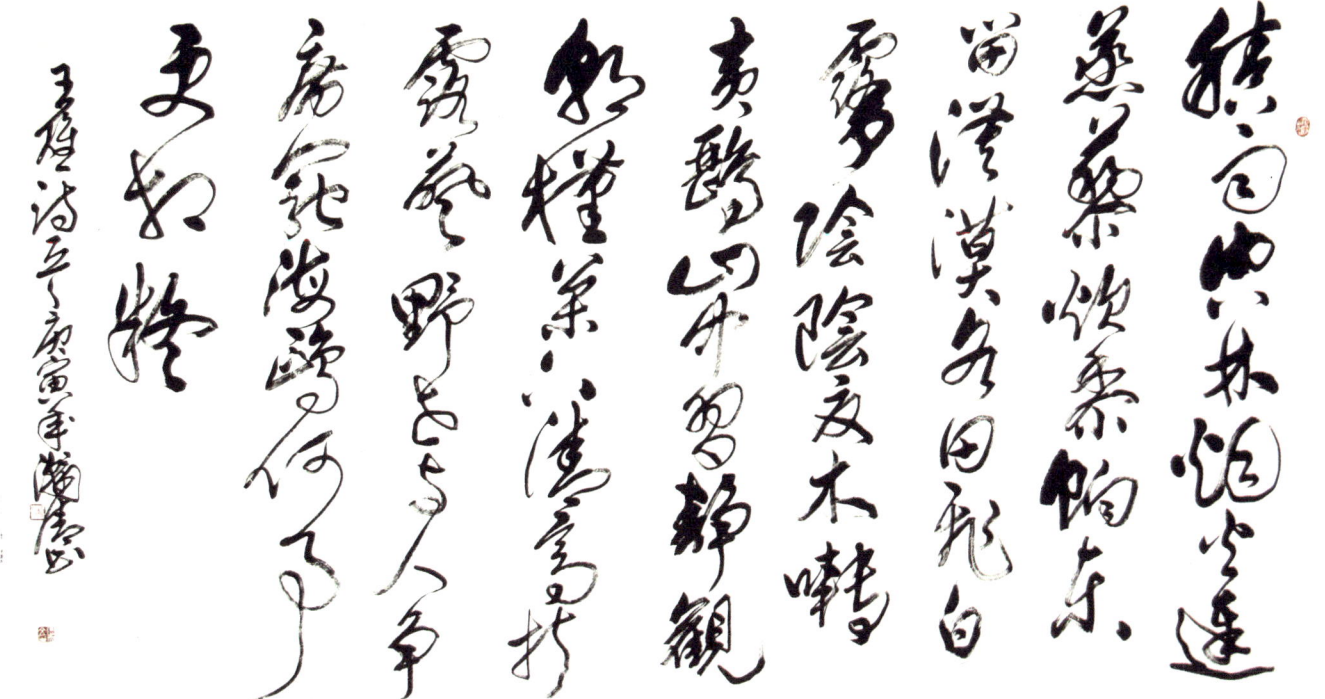

《王维诗一首》 *A Poem by Wang Wei*

中国当代书画名家作品收藏指南 | **247**

周 彬
ZHOU BIN

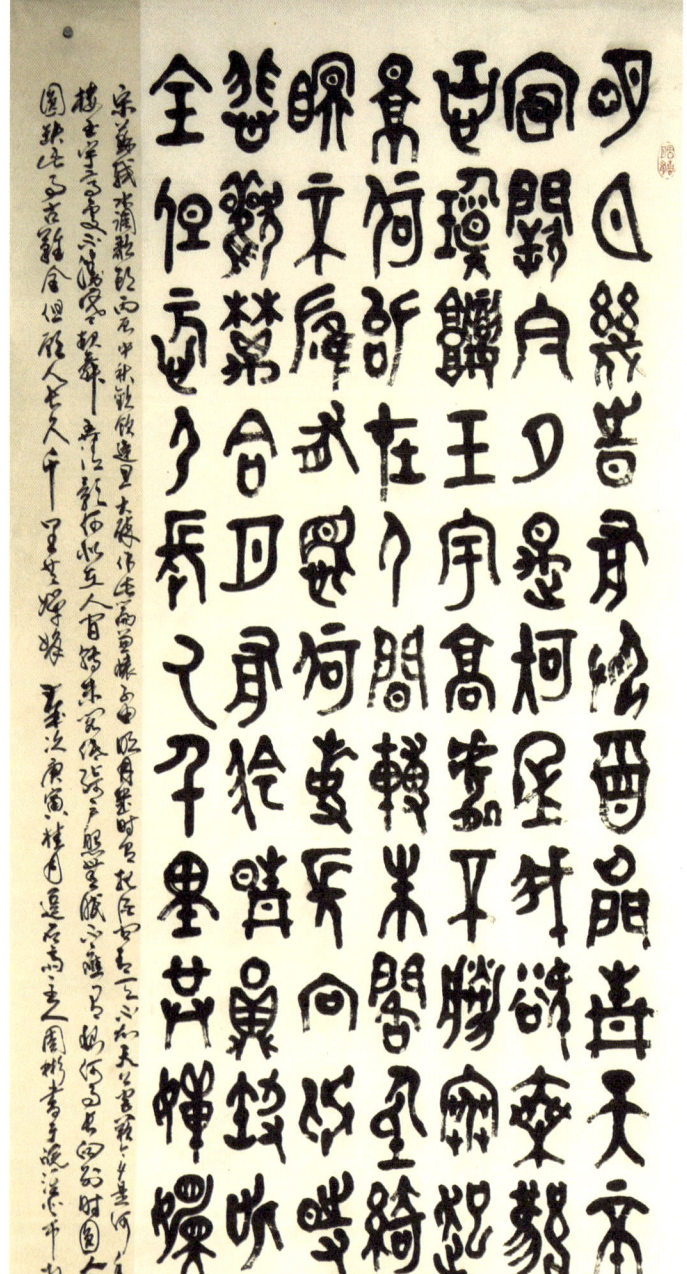

《苏轼 水调歌头》179*75 *Remembering Su Zhe by Su Shi*

周　彬　1940年出生，安徽省淮北市人，淮北市书协会员，淮北市书画家协会会员，中国老年书画艺术编辑部艺术委员会会员。

润笔价格：2000~3000/平尺
供收藏家参考

Zhou Bin, born in 1940 in Huaibei, Anhui Province, is a member of Huaibei Calligraphers Association, of Huaibei Calligrapher and Painter Association, and of Arts Committee of China Calligraphy and Painting Art for the Aged.

Reference price: RMB2000-3000 per square feet

周克民 ZHOU KEMIN

《行书 赞龙歌》 97*180
In Praise of Dragon (Semi-cursive Script) 97*180

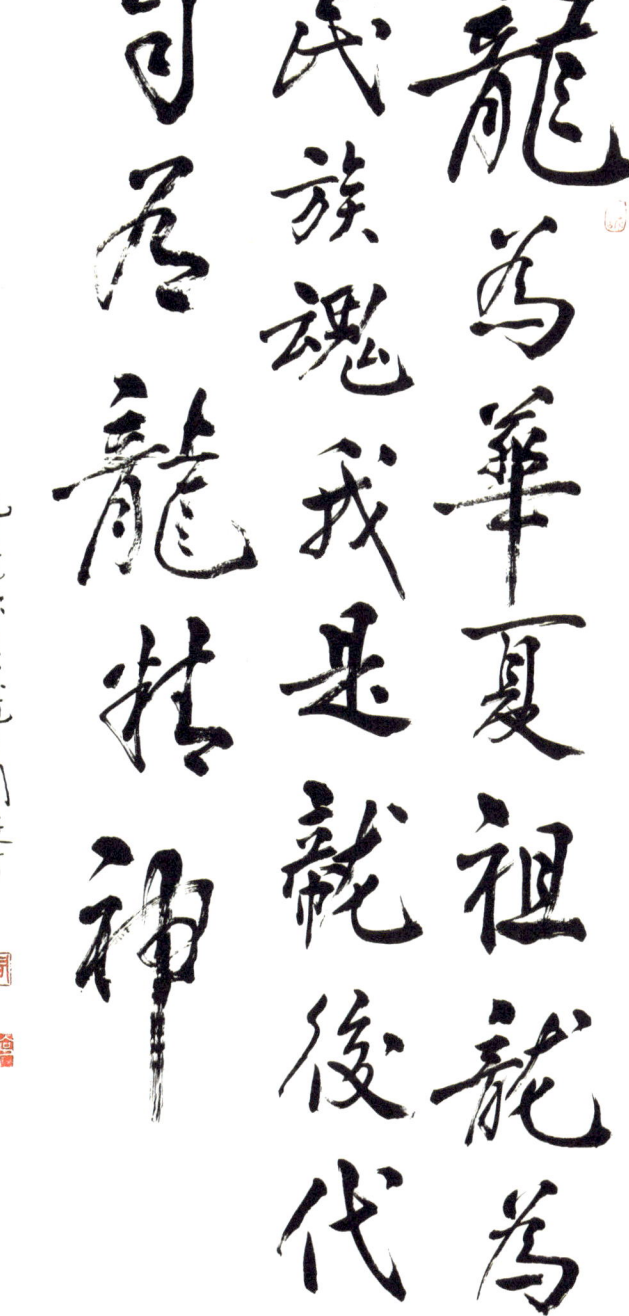

周克民 1954年12月生，研究生文化，中国书法家协会会员。

润格：3000~4000/平尺
供收藏家参考

Zhou Kemin, born in December in 1954 and a Master's degree holder, is a member of China Calligraphers Association.

Reference price: RMB3000-4000 per square feet

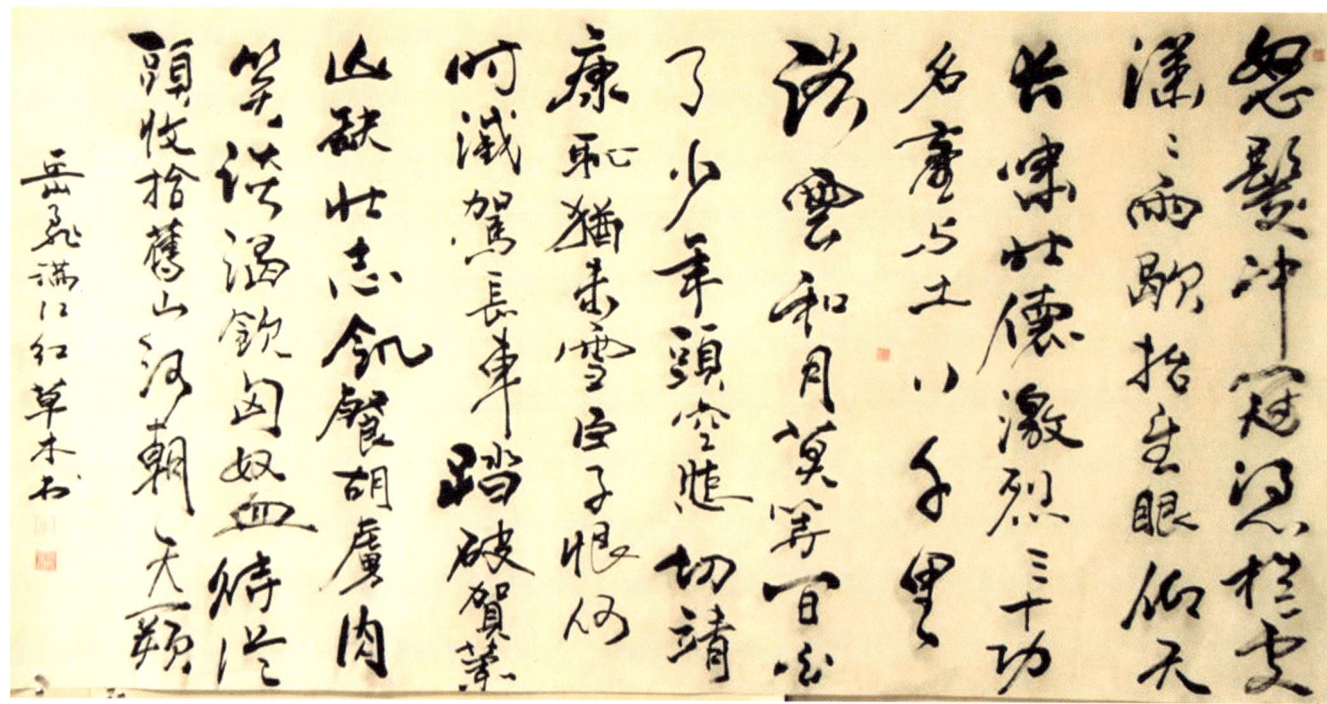

《行草 满江红》 *Man Jiang Hong (Semi-cursive Script)*

李红星
ZHOU BIN

李红星 北京京洲翰墨书画院执行院长，中国书画家协会会员。

润笔价格：3000~4000/平尺
供收藏家参考

Li Hongxing is Executive President of Beijing Jingzhou Hanmo Calligraphy and Painting Gallery and member of China Calligrapher and Painter Association.

Reference price: RMB3000-4000 per square feet

后 序

文化产业是市场经济条件下繁荣发展社会主义文化的重要载体，党中央、国务院高度重视发展这一产业，为此采取了一系列政策措施，深入推进文化体制改革，加快推动文化产业发展。2009 年 7 月 22 日，国务院总理温家宝主持召开国务院常务会议，讨论并原则通过了《文化产业振兴规划》。中国书画是我国传统文化的重要组成部分，是我们的国粹，书画产业是我国文化产业的一个重要方面。在当前国内外的新形势下，书画市场的繁荣对于满足人民群众多样化、多层次、多方面精神文化需求，以及扩大内需、推动经济结构调整，都具有十分重要的意义。

总的来看，目前我国的书画产业呈现出健康向上、蓬勃发展的良好态势，正在成为推动社会主义文化大发展、大繁荣的重要引擎和经济发展新的增长点。但同时要看到，我国书画产业的发展水平还不高、书画市场还不太规范，这不但与人民群众日益增长的精神文化需求、日趋完善的社会主义市场经济体制不相适应，而且与我国对外开放不断扩大的新形势也不和谐。

为了适应当前国内外文化市场的新形势，由东方水墨文化有限公司和中央编译出版社联合出版发行的《中国当代书画名家作品收藏指南》系列丛书第一卷与大家见面了。编者本着艺术、学术至上的原则来选择书画家和作品，力争把本丛书打造成书画收藏界的经典之作，给广大的书画研究和创作者，以及投资者、收藏者以参考借鉴。同时我们还会给该书所收录的有实力、有潜力的书画家提供一系列的书画经纪服务。我们坚信，通过不懈地努力，本丛书的问世将会为书画市场科学良性产业链的形成大有裨益。

本书的出版发行得到社会各界的帮助和支持，在此一并感谢。囿于各种条件，书中纰漏及不足之处在所难免，恳请读者不吝赐教，提出您的宝贵建议，以便我们在以后工作中及时改正。

图书在版编目（CIP）数据

中国当代书画名家作品收藏指南 / 孟云飞著. —北京：中央编译出版社，2011.5
ISBN 978-7-5117-0865-6

Ⅰ.①中… Ⅱ.①孟… Ⅲ.①汉字—书法—收藏—中国—指南
②中国画—收藏—中国—指南 Ⅳ.①G894-62

中国版本图书馆CIP数据核字（2011）第076552号

中国当代书画名家作品收藏指南

出 版 人：	和 龑
责任编辑：	何嗣虎
出版发行：	中央编译出版社
地　　址：	北京西单西斜街36号（100032）
电　　话：	(010) 66509360（总编室）　(010) 66509366（编辑室）
	(010) 66509364（发行部）　(010) 66509618（读者服务部）
	(010) 66161011（团购部）　(010) 66130345（网络销售部）
网　　址：	www.cctpbook.com
经　　销：	全国新华书店
印　　刷：	北京国邦印刷有限责任公司
开　　本：	889毫米×1194毫米　1/16
字　　数：	80千字
印　　张：	16
版　　次：	2011年6月第1版第1次印刷
定　　价：	980.00元

本社常年法律顾问：北京大成律师事务所首席顾问律师　鲁哈达
凡有印装质量问题，本社负责调换。电话：(010) 66509618